"*Born to Perform*...touches at the heart of what it takes to succeed. Gerard Hartmann is an unsung hero with a unique ability to heal, motivate and instil self-belief in those he treats."
— *Dame Kelly Holmes, double Olympic champion, 800 metres and 1,500 metres*

"Rugby was professional, but my body was not! Gerard Hartmann's hands were needed to bridge that gap... In *Born to Perform* he uses those same hands for more gentle work: a candid portrayal of what made him the foremost Irish triathlete and a world-leading physical therapist."
— *Keith Wood, former international rugby player*

"For those of you lucky enough to meet Gerard Hartmann on your journey through life, you will instantly recognise his voice and infectious enthusiasm in his inspiring book *Born to Perform*. For those of you who haven't, prepare to meet a very special man when you read this book. Truly a one-off."
— *Paul Galvin, Kerry senior football team; Footballer of the Year 2009*

"...an inspirational book that touches at the very heart of why sport is such an integral part of many people's lives. Gerard Hartmann...shares his unique life story which captures the very essence of the value of sport and of the pursuit of excellence."
— *Seán Óg Ó hAilpín, Cork senior hurling team; Hurler of the Year 2004*

"Passionate, honest, gifted and inspiring. Not only has Gerard touched the lives of so many people...he transformed them. His positive attitude is infectious. A true champion of life."
— *Senator Eamonn Coghlan, three-time Olympian and former 5,000-metre world champion*

"In this compelling read, the enthusiasm and grá for life of Gerard Hartmann penetrates to the core of your spirit just as deeply as his healing hands do for his athletes."
— *Mickey Harte, Manager, Tyrone senior football team*

"This book explores the mindset and common threads of success in sport and life and leaves you with the clear idea...that excellence is perseverance in disguise."
— *Marcus O'Sullivan, Head Athletics Coach, Vill*
three-time world indoor 1,500-metre champion

"[Gerard Hartmann's] wisdom and knowledge on how the mind and body work together in healing is unique...He gives an injured player or athlete the confidence needed to get back to his best. *Born to Perform* shows much of his uniqueness and expertise."
— *Lar Corbett, Tipperary senior hurling team; Hurler of the Year 2010*

"*Born to Perform* is a must-read for those seeking excellence in a competitive world."
— *Jack O'Connor, Manager, Kerry senior football team*

"In *Born to Perform*, Gerard has captured the essence of the 'soul of sport' from every angle. A must-read to see what it takes to reach gold medal performances."
— *Cyle Sage, former professional triathlete; two-time US Olympic Developmental Coach of the Year for Triathlon.*

"An inspirational read that challenges the competitor in all of us to be the best we can possibly be."
— *Brian Cody, Manager, Kilkenny senior hurling team*

"[*Born to Perform*] will inspire people to overcome adversity and proves that positivity, love and a `never give up' attitude will bring you far in life."
— *James McGee, Irish international tennis player*

"*Born to Perform* is a very inspirational story about a man who never settled with good, but kept pushing for excellence. I read the book during one weekend and it stole lots of needed sleep from my training regime. Gerard Hartmann inspires me to be the best I can be."
— *Lisa Norden (Sweden), world triathlon champion 2010*

"In *Born to Perform*, [Gerard Hartmann] openly shares his story of how sport shaped his life and, through his gift, how he shaped the lives of so many sportspeople."
— *Lornah Kiplagat (the Netherlands/Kenya), three-time world champion in the half marathon; world cross country champion*

"Running through my mind are thoughts of all the races I ran. On my chest are medals from the races I won. In my heart is gratitude to Gerard Hartmann for helping make my dreams come true. I am very honoured to be a part of this wonderful book."
— *Douglas Wakiihuri (Kenya), world gold medallist and Olympic silver medallist in the marathon*

To: David Cahill,

Born to Perform

How Sport Has Shaped My Life

Best Wishes,
Gerard Hartmann

Gerard Hartmann

ORPEN PRESS

First published in 2011 by Orpen Press
Lonsdale House
Avoca Avenue
Blackrock
Co. Dublin
Ireland

e-mail: info@orpenpress.com
www.orpenpress.com

Reprinted in 2012
Copyright © Gerard Hartmann, 2011

ISBN: 978-1-871305-27-2 PBK
978-1-871305-30-2 HBK

A catalogue record for this book is available from the British Library.

*Royalties from the sale of this book
will be donated to Console (www.console.ie),
the national charity for supporting people in
suicidal crisis and those bereaved by suicide.*

Photos on back cover depict Seán Óg Ó hAilpín and Kelly Holmes
in the Hartmann International Sports Injury Clinic,
Limerick, in 2005 and 1999 respectively.

Printed in the UK by the MPG Books Group

This book is dedicated to
my parents Patrick and Thecla Hartmann,
and my wife Dr Diane Bennis,
and my sons Patrick Tadgh Hartmann
and Michael Gerard Hartmann.

About the Author

Since 1991 Gerard Hartmann has worked as a physical therapist with many of the world's greatest athletes, including over 60 Olympic medal winners, plus numerous world champions and world record holders.

He has served on national teams with the United States, Ireland and Great Britain at the past five Olympic Games, and has been appointed physical therapist to the Irish Olympic Team for the 2012 London Olympic Games.

He operates Hartmann International Sports Injury Clinic at the University of Limerick, and also at the High Altitude Training Centre in Iten, Kenya.

In his own sporting career, Gerard was the first known Irishman to compete in a triathlon. He was also among Ireland's first triathlon champions, winning seven national senior championships from 1984 to 1991.

He represented Ireland in European, World Championship and Hawaii Ironman events – and is thus recognised as one of the pioneers of the sport of triathlon. He was also responsible for founding the Limerick Triathlon Club and starting the Kilkee Triathlon – also known as "the Hell of the West" – which remains the longest running triathlon in Ireland.

FOREWORD

By Frank O'Mara, two-time world indoors 3,000-metre champion; three-time Irish Olympian 1984, 1988 and 1992

The great American industrialist Henry Ford once said, "Whether you think that you can or that you can't, you're usually right."

I first met Gerard Hartmann when he was thirteen years old, and even then he firmly believed that he could. His self-confidence and enthusiasm are two of his most endearing qualities.

I had known of Gerard for many years before I met him. His mother and my father grew up in the neighbouring villages of Kilkishen and Tulla, Co. Clare, and came from staunch GAA families.

Our first encounter was at a Limerick Athletic Club training session at the LPYMA grounds on the Ennis Road, directly across from Gerard's family home. Gerard bounded into the grounds that night full of youthful ebullience and quickly established himself as a force to be reckoned with.

In Gerard's second season of competitive running, he moved up from the 100-metre and 400-metre sprint events to the 800 metres and broke my North Munster Schools record by three seconds, running it in two minutes and nine seconds. His record, I believe, stood for twenty-one years.

He was a big lad with lots of talent, and he was always eager to race, famously winning the 800 metres, 1,500 metres, 3,000 metres and 1,500 metres steeplechase in the Munster Championships in 1978. He broke two records in the process.

He added to his reputation for flair by always sporting the latest sports gear. He had a fascination with running shoes and track spikes.

While many of us considered him overzealous, those of us who knew him better could see that he had an enquiring mind and an extraordinary attention to detail, with an equal measure of enthusiasm and a desire to be the best.

He kept a meticulous account of every training session and recorded his heart rate and weight daily. His training diaries were sprinkled with inspirational quotes and adorned with motivational pictures of his favourite athletes such as Lasse Virén, Eamonn Coghlan and Sebastian Coe.

Amazingly, he was always willing to share his knowledge about training and performance with fellow competitors.

Gerard joined the exodus of Irish junior athletes of the 1970s to the US on an athletic scholarship. He enrolled as a freshman at McNeese State University in Louisiana in 1979. There he was introduced to the arduous cycle of injury and therapy.

Later, as college teammates at the University of Arkansas, Gerard helped me survive a year-long, almost career-ending injury. Even before he had professional training he was learning about sports physiology, injury treatment and rehabilitation. He had a contagiously positive disposition. His company alone always lifted your spirits.

Over the years we both had more than our fair share of injuries. I stuck to Gerard's coat tails during those years. He was always at the vanguard of treatment protocols, constantly exploring new, and often radical, approaches. During one particularly adventuresome period, we endured deep tissue manipulation applied by a high-powered hose while submerged underwater. Gerard understands the frustrations of those demented by injury and desperate to recover. He has been there and through it himself.

Gerard was one of the world's leading triathletes when his career tragically ended. He crashed and broke his hip cycling at 50 kilometres per hour on a north Florida road and was airlifted to hospital. It was a devastating end to his competitive athletic career.

Fortuitously, for all those he has treated since, Gerard channelled his considerable energy into his burgeoning career as a physical therapist. He immerses himself in every individual's predicament and partners with them in a comprehensive rehabilitative programme that includes direct treatment of the injury, strengthening and stretching exercises, and a fitness maintenance plan. He convinces you that, not only will you recover, but that when you do you will exceed previous performance levels. He never wants you to experience the frustration of unfulfilled promise or the disappointment of a career interruption.

When Gerard asked me to be his best man at his wedding to Diane in October 2006, I was honoured. When he contacted me and told me about the book he was writing and how he wanted me to write the foreword, I was equally honoured.

Gerard does nothing by half measures. When I read the initial manuscript of *Born to Perform*, it inspired me so much that I wanted my son to read it. Gerard wrote the book his own way and in his own style, and his voice is identifiable straightaway. It is a powerful life story that will inspire people to believe that they can reach their true potential in sport and in life.

After all these years knowing Gerard Hartmann, I know that, not only does he believe he can, but he also believes *you* can. And, as Henry Ford would say, he is right.

August 2011

FOREWORD

By Sonia O'Sullivan, world gold medallist and Olympic silver medallist in the 5,000 metres; three-time European champion and two-time world cross country champion.

Flight QF9: Melbourne via Singapore to London.

I never look forward to long-haul flights, but they've got to be done. I was travelling to London for the Chefs de Mission seminar in preparation for the London 2012 Olympic Games, where I will be the Chef de Mission to the Irish Olympic Team.

Gerard had sent me a copy of *Born to Perform*, so I saved it until the flight, knowing that it would shorten my journey.

I really did not know what to expect from *Born to Perform*, except that I know that anything Gerard does he does extremely well, with no half measures. I was looking forward all week to burying myself in this new book. Once I started reading, I knew it would be nearly impossible to put down.

Gerard has been my trusted physical therapist for twenty years. More importantly, he is one of my very good friends. He has always been there for me through my highs and lows as an athlete. It's not just that he is the best physio I know; it's the positivity and belief he brings out in me. He is really a special person.

When I was a schoolgirl, I remember watching Gerard on RTÉ defending his Irish triathlon title year after year. I saw articles and photographs of him in the *Irish Runner* and *Marathon* magazines, but I never knew his passion as an athlete.

I've known Gerard since 1992. It was at this time that he really found his gift, when his career as an athlete was cut short through injury.

Born to Perform gives a great insight into the sport of triathlon and Ironman events, and into Gerard's life as a world-class athlete.

I understand now the passion Gerard has for his daily work. He took his sporting passion and work ethic and re-invented himself as a physical therapist, determined to be the best he could possibly be. Gerard is known universally as having a special ability and as one of the best physical therapists in the world.

He knows the commitment required to be a world-class athlete. He has experienced success and disappointment along the way as an athlete himself, and this allows him to impart his passion and motivation to every person that walks into his clinic. Gerard is the most positive, energising person I know. His experience and knowledge allows him to diagnose an injury, and assist athletes to work through a plan of treatment.

Whenever I have gone to Gerard with injuries, he always makes the diagnosis and then asserts the positives. His treatments are never easy, but they are always worthwhile. It's never about what you can't do, always about what you can do.

I would say that he is the most pro-active person that an athlete from any sport can have in their corner. When it looks like their back is up against the wall and they are facing the biggest challenge of their life, he is the person who helps make dreams come true.

I would like to thank Gerard for all the positive energy and support he has given to me throughout my career, even now when I am trying to get out and run, to enjoy the freedom and joy that running gives to me each day.

Gerard shares his passion and enthusiasm for sport and life in *Born to Perform*. It is a book full of important sporting and professional life lessons from the life of a remarkable person. The stories and insights that Gerard shares are inspirational.

Above all, *Born to Perform* will empower readers to believe in themselves and to strive to be the best they can be.

August 2011

PREFACE

In November 2010 the great Kilkenny hurler Henry Shefflin looked up at me from the physio table, where I had him pinned down with both thumbs dug deep into the back of his knee, and said: "There's a great book in you. When are you going to write it?"

I answered with the question, "Well, Henry, when are we going to see your book?"

He responded, "I suppose after I've won a few more All-Ireland hurling titles with Kilkenny. Ten would be nice. But, seriously, you've got to do a book, Gerard, you have some great stories to tell."

Sometimes, all one needs is a nudge from someone who they really respect. Henry's encouragement stayed fresh in my mind and, weeks later, another friend, Kenneth Gasque, the director of La Santa Sports Complex in Lanzarote, hit the same note with the comment, "Gerard, you must write the book on the sport of triathlon in its infancy. You are one of the pioneers of the sport – you must do the book."

So I promised Kenneth that I would write the book. In fact, I travelled to Lanzarote on my own in February 2011 for eight days, with the sole purpose of spending ten to twelve hours writing each day – by hand, no less. I immersed myself in the project with greater mission and zeal than preparing for any Ironman triathlon. Rather than ending up with sore legs, I sustained writer's cramp and costochondritis (inflammation of the ribs) from being bent over writing for hours on end.

I dialled into my memory bank and creative self, putting my heart and soul into writing this book. In the end, I came away with about 300 A4 pages, all handwritten, and this became the makings of the story of how sport has shaped my life. I gave it my all, in the spirit of the Olympic ethos Higher, Faster, Stronger.

I called my good friend Ian O'Riordan, one of the leading sports writers with the *Irish Times*, and told him that I was over in Lanzarote for eight days writing my book. Ian responded, "Wow, that's a big challenge, Gerard, and a big commitment." On my return, I showed Ian the handwritten pages, and straightaway he supported and encouraged me.

So what is *Born to Perform* all about?

Well, first, it is my life story, from my young years, when I was suspended from school for being a troublemaker, to six years later getting an athletic scholarship to the US as a runner. It tells of my athletic dreams and drive, and how I became the first Irish person to participate in a triathlon, a new sport at the time. I became seven-time Irish triathlon champion and competed internationally as Ireland's champion of the new sport – until tragedy struck and I broke my hip in a freak cycling accident that terminated my competitive career.

The book tells how, out of depression and despair, I came to reach the top of my profession as a physical therapist. Working with over 60 Olympic medal winners, world champions and some of the best sportspeople in the world has been a unique experience, which I share in this book.

The book also gives some advice on dealing with adversity and with stress, and how to perform and excel in sport and in life. Sport shaped my life and I share what I feel are the reasons for this. I want to inspire people to "fly higher to see more", to empower people to use and maximise their God-given talents.

I have always followed my star and done the things in life that I wanted to do, not what someone else wanted for me. For the most part, it has been an extremely rewarding, exciting and happy journey.

So many people have guided and helped me through my fifty years of life. I have many friends throughout the world – there are too many to mention. To every one of you I wish to express my sincere thanks and appreciation for you being part of my life.

Thanks to my mother Thecla for being my biggest supporter and my dad Patrick for allowing me the freedom to expand my wings and find my own path in life. To my sisters Leonie, Thecla and Helga – thank you for your love, friendship and support.

To my late grandmother Nora Deasy, who encouraged me to "Keep up that running – it will take you far." She attended all my All-Ireland Triathlon victories and was waiting at the finish line in sun and rain.

A special heartfelt thank you to my beautiful wife Diane, whose love, encouragement, support, loyalty and belief in me is never-ending. And to Diane's parents, Agnes and Tadg, for being so supportive. My two-and-a-half-year-old son Patrick Hartmann Jnr is the boss of the house – thank you for bringing fun and joy into my life. My second son Michael Gerard Hartmann Jnr was born at around the same time as this book was published, in November 2011.

I am grateful to Ger Keane, the smiling man from Castleisland, Co. Kerry, my colleague at Hartmann International Sports Injury Clinic. I was lucky to find a kindred spirit to work alongside who has a similar drive and passion to be the very best. Karena O'Brien keeps the office running smoothly and I appreciate her support in making the clinic a dream come true.

To Frank O'Mara, my lifelong friend – thank you for always being there for me and for writing a foreword to the book.

Sonia O'Sullivan is almost another sister to me; a friend for life. Thanks, Sonia, for your support for the book and for taking the time and energy to write a foreword. You are Ireland's greatest champion.

Ian O'Riordan encouraged me in the early stages of writing, and was kind enough to give me valuable editorial guidance. He's also written a piece on triathlon in Ireland, which is at the end of the book. So, thank you, Ian, for your belief in me and in the book.

To Gerard O'Connor and Elizabeth Brennan at Orpen Press – thank you both for working with me towards publishing this book. Also, thank you to Pery Square Business College in Limerick, who typed up the original manuscript.

Finally, to all those who are down and struggling in life – I hope you will see opportunity and the world in a far better light after reading this book.

Gerard Hartmann
February 2012

CONTENTS

Contents

<u>1</u>

A Hard Fall

I am lying in a hospital bed, bleary-eyed and semi-conscious, drugged to the limit, drifting in and out of this world. I feel suspended in a surreal trance of repeated bad dreams, against the backdrop of one reality: it is all over. My identity has been shattered. I am nothing now, another accident statistic – one of the many people who, in a split second, see their lives changed forever, without any warning.

A few hours earlier I had been cycling along Highway 441, just outside Gainesville, Florida. I had my triathlon time trial bike in top gear and I was speeding along, doing the hard interval training: 1 mile in 2 minutes – that's 30 miles per hour – then coasting for a minute to recover, to allow my heart rate to decrease from 180 beats per minute to 130, and then stomping on the pedals again at full effort for another mile. I would do this ten times.

Two more to go. Out of the saddle at full strength, to power the machine up to over 30 miles per hour, then tucking low onto the handlebars to get aerodynamic to slice through as much wind resistance as possible.

Then, in that moment when I was concentrating so hard on the effort, my front wheel hit an armadillo that was scampering unknowingly across the road. Within the blink of an eye, my bicycle and I were sent flying through the air, totally out of control. All the while, I was sensing cars whizzing past at 70 miles per hour. My first and last bit of fortune was that I fell inwards onto the road's shoulder, rather than out into the busy traffic – and certain death.

I hit the road surface with an unmerciful bang, landing straight down on my right hip, still clipped into my bike pedals. Lying in agony, bloodied and unable to move, shivering and shaking with shock on the melting road in 90°F heat, car after car began to stop and people towered over me as I lay helpless on the road. The impact had sliced my hip and split it cleanly into two pieces.

Dr Phillip Parr, the orthopaedic surgeon who had operated on me for four hours, stopped in to visit the day after my surgery. He was an avid runner who participated in numerous marathons and triathlon events, and in that regard we shared a common bond.

His sporting dream was to participate in the most famous and gruelling of all triathlons, the Hawaii Ironman, although he failed to qualify. I was something of a superstar in his eyes, a world-class triathlete; one of the top fifteen in the world; an athlete who only yesterday was in the prime of his career, yet now lying helpless in a hospital bed.

Dr Parr stood by my bedside and explained that, had I not been airlifted by helicopter to the North Florida Regional Medical Center and undergone emergency surgery, avascular necrosis would have set in. The blood supply to my hip would have been cut off within hours and I would have lost my leg. "Gerard," he said, "you are one lucky man. I have put a Richardson compression screw, a fixation plate and four screws into your leg. The good news is that we saved it; the bad news is that you will probably never run again."

Ten days earlier in Sligo, on Sunday, August 18, 1991, I won a seventh National Triathlon title. I covered the Half Ironman event – that's a 1.2-mile swim, a 56-mile bike ride and 13.1-mile run – in 4 hours and 28 seconds, and it was the closest I'd ever come to feeling like poetry in motion.

I exited the water in first place and ran up the beach at Rosses Point, leaving my so-called weakest event (swimming) behind, along with over 400 fellow competitors. It was their last chance that day to see my back.

I stormed around the 56-mile bike course in 2 hours 17 minutes, over 7 minutes quicker than the next fastest triathlete. Cormac McCann from Belfast, an Olympic cyclist, recorded the fastest time for the bike leg of the relay, only having to do the cycle. He rode fully equipped with a specialist time trial bike, complete with rear disc wheel, and yet he was two minutes slower than my time.

I faced the 13.1-mile run after dismounting the bike with such a lead that all I had to do was treat the run like a training jaunt. Professional cyclists hone their fitness to a peak to achieve that unique feeling of body and machine being in unison. That day, my composite Kestrel bike and I breezed around the roads of Sligo and Leitrim as if together we had been turbocharged – an unstoppable force of body and machine.

To have experienced that feeling just once was worth all the hard training and sacrifices. Often sportspeople will not win any major event, but an experience like that brings an inner satisfaction far more meaningful and worthy than any medal or trophy.

After the Sligo victory, and the day before returning to Florida, where three months earlier I had qualified as a physical therapist, I was in a fancy French restaurant in Dublin being interviewed over dinner by the sports journalist Paul Kimmage.

I was to be the subject of his big feature for the *Sunday Tribune*. Paul was a former Irish champion and Tour de France cyclist, and understood human performance both in the dedicated purist sense and also the trained but chemically enhanced sense, which he himself had been familiar with. He "spat in the soup" and broke his secret and silence in his book *Rough Ride*.

Paul invited me to Dublin – and the *Sunday Tribune* flew me up from Shannon Airport. I knew very little about Paul except that he was a retired professional cyclist, good enough in his day to race with Seán Kelly, Stephen Roche and Martin Earley, and was now one of the top sports feature writers in the country. I reasoned that being invited by Paul Kimmage to Dublin was evidence that the press were finally following triathlon and taking my status on the international stage seriously. Paul apologised during our conversation for not travelling to Limerick to do the interview, explaining that he had just got in a couple of hours earlier from Lucerne in Switzerland where he was covering Niall O'Toole competing in the Single Scull event at the World Rowing Championships.

Every 30 minutes, Paul would flick out the tape from his old-style tape recorder on the dining table, turn the tape around to the other side or insert a new tape, and continue the interview. Towards the end of a long and amiable interview, a serious frown and sternness suddenly covered Paul's face. I straightaway sensed he had something he wanted to address. He looked uncomfortable.

For almost three hours I had spilled out my heart to Paul. I shared my passion for triathlon to a fellow sportsman and shown him my personal training diaries which documented my training, day after day, week after week, with few if any recovery days, sometimes doing four training sessions in a single day. Paul looked me in the eye, and the fellow athlete who I so easily identified with was now wearing only one cap – that of a journalist looking for the kill.

Maybe this guy Hartmann is like I was, he must have thought, selling a big lie and performing on the juice. Getting straight to the point, he stated, "I'm not going to believe for one moment that you are training and competing at that level in this most demanding sport without taking drugs."

I tried to assure Paul that I never doped, that the pharmaceutical company that distributed Pharmaton in Ireland supplied me with a one-a-day multi-vitamin, in fact gave me a year's supply, and, other than wholesome food, that was all that fuelled my engine. Paul was not convinced, and I knew it. I knew it by his body language, by the lack of sincerity in his handshake when we said goodbye. Maybe he was tormented by his own drug taking and wanted another dream to be spoiled. But my dream was real. Everything I had ever achieved in triathlon was achieved by desire, passion, perseverance, enthusiasm and a work ethic which ultimately far outweighed whatever physical talents I had been blessed with.

Yet, here I now was, in a hospital bed in Florida, pumped up with drugs alright but for all the wrong reasons. I had a catheter in my right arm and was receiving an infusion of Demerol and Phenergan through a drip, to kill the pain and protect against post-surgery infection. Every six hours, I would receive two injections into my backside and also take an oral stool softener because all the medication was clogging up my digestive system.

I needed to speak to Paul Kimmage. He was running his big interview that coming Sunday and I needed to put a stop to it. My competitive sporting career was over.

I was going to be in hospital for two weeks and on crutches for a further sixteen, and after that I would have to learn how to walk again. Back in Ireland, the best sports journalist was penning a 5,000-word article on my athletic exploits, but I was not an athlete at this point in time. I couldn't even piss straight and had to piddle into a jar next to the bed. It was five days after the accident before the physical therapist showed me how to get out of bed and use a Zimmer frame to walk six steps to the toilet.

I did not want the whole country to know about my career ending in tragedy, not just yet anyway. It was too sudden, too raw. I needed to get my head around it and I had nobody to talk to. I knew if Paul Kimmage's feature article was printed, and only after that word got out that I was half crippled in hospital, the fall would be even harder. I needed time to figure out what I was going to do, and how.

I phoned Paul from my hospital bed.

"Paul, Gerard Hartmann here. I want you to pull the feature you are writing on me for this weekend."

Silence at the end of the line – and then: "It's written; it's going to press on Sunday. Why, is there a problem?"

"No, no, not really, but I'm asking you not to print it as I've decided to take a break from triathlon…I'm not sure if my body can take all the hard training anymore."

Silence again. I'm not sure who put down the phone first.

I imagined Paul on his phone back home, saying, "Bollocks…I knew the prick was on drugs. He's probably in trouble now. Guilt has set in and he wants a way out."

I sank back into my bed and started to cry. Suddenly I started to question everything, all the whys – why I couldn't even tell the truth to Paul Kimmage. But it was too early. A part of me knew it was over, and yet another part of my mind had already dialled back into planning training strategies for next season's triathlons.

I had won seven National Triathlon titles – and my mind was still in that racing mode. Get the leg sorted, rehabilitate and drive on for three more seasons. Make it ten All-Ireland titles!

Triathlon was my life. I was addicted alright, because it was my drug. It was what I lived for, dreamed of, and what I ate and slept. Deep down a part of me knew this was all over now, but still it was going to take time and healing to sort out how to deal with it, and how to present it to the world, to my family, to my friends and to Paul Kimmage. More pressing would be its effect on me internally, how I would deal with the death of my life as an international athlete, and saving myself from depression and despair.

All I knew at that point was that triathlon would have to be replaced with something meaningful that I was just as passionate about – and replaced fast. At the time, I could not figure out why triathlon meant everything to me – but over the years I have come to understand. In the 21 years in my profession as a physical therapist, I have met many sportspeople from so many different sports, from GAA footballers and hurlers to rugby players, tennis players, cyclists, runners, swimmers and triathletes, and seen how sport is also the thing that defines their lives, their identity.

Tipperary hurling legend Johnny Leahy, who I worked with rehabilitating him through his second anterior cruciate ligament injury, captured the very heart and soul of sport when he said, after Tipperary won the All-Ireland Hurling final in 1991:

> It's a great honour to put on that county jersey. I don't think money can buy it. It's where you come from, where you were born. It's what you've grown up with. To wear that jersey you are very lucky. To run on the field representing your people is an incredible feeling. To win something is unreal. To play and win something for your county is phenomenal.

At even the most basic level, human beings want to succeed, to be part of something unique and special. The fellowship of sport is a universal language that binds people and gives their lives meaning and purpose. One of the end results is that sport can become the person's life, their all or nothing, and perhaps we should never even question why. The answer is to just enjoy it, because tomorrow may never come.

2

The Early Days of Triathlon

I am walking along the promenade in Puerto del Carmen in Lanzarote. It's January 1, 2011, and it's a walk I have done on the first day of the New Year for the past five years. By the shore front stands a sculpture and commemorative plate celebrating the first-ever Lanzarote Ironman Triathlon, held on the island on 30 May 1992. It was the brainchild of my good friend Kenneth Gasque, the director for many years of La Santa Sports Centre in Lanzarote.

Kenneth and I first met on the Island of Hawaii in 1985, when we were both competing in the Ironman World Triathlon Championship – that's the full 2.4-mile swim, 112-mile cycle and 26.2-mile marathon run. When Kenneth Gasque crossed the finish line on Ali'i Drive on October 26, 1985, he became the first Danish person to complete the Hawaii Ironman. He went on to start the first triathlon in Lanzarote and was also the originator of the Volcano Triathlon, along with the now famous Lanzarote Ironman of which he still acts as race director.

Kenneth and I meet up regularly, and reflect on and banter about the innocence of those early days in what we both know were the formative years of the triathlon. As I stand admiring the commemorative plaque, I reflect on the uniqueness of having played a part in pioneering and developing the sport of triathlon. Kenneth was the one who nudged me to put pen to paper and document some of this story – the story of triathlon in its infancy.

Many people have no idea of how the sport of triathlon first developed, how it evolved and what it was like in the early days, especially in Ireland. It was my life, and in many ways the only life I lived from

1984 to 1991. In some ways, then, I feel obliged to give an insight into the wonderful sport of triathlon in its early years.

In the mid-to-late 1970s, *The Superstars* was an international made-for-television competition for which famous sports stars from all over the world converged annually in the Bahamas. The idea was simple: the competition pitted some of the great sports stars and sporting heroes against one another for the coveted title of World Superstar Champion.

The champion of the Irish Superstars competition received an all-expenses-paid trip to the Bahamas to compete internationally. The Irish contest was thus televised as an exciting one-hour competition, shown at prime time – and not surprisingly it achieved a maximum viewership rating at the time.

The RTÉ crew then covered the Irish champion superstar competing against the best in the world in the Bahamas. Memories of the great Olympic 400-metre hurdles champion Edwin Moses going head-to-head against Kerry football star Pat Spillane, participating in five events – ranging from an obstacle course with climbing wall and tightrope beam to track cycling, archery, running, throwing and lifting heavy objects – still come easily to mind. It was spectacular television, showing the fittest athletes in the world doing combat in exotic settings.

By 1982, RTÉ executive producer Justin Nelson had witnessed *The Superstars* reach its pinnacle, then realised the ship was leaking. It had outgrown itself, or else it simply had had its day. Justin looked at other options and by chance stumbled across an ABC TV production from the US showing the first-ever televised Hawaii Ironman event.

The history books show that this took place after a retired naval commander Captain John Collins found himself in a bar room argument with his friends over who was the most fit – the long-distance swimmer, the endurance cyclist or the marathon runner. Was it Mark Spitz, the nine-time Olympic swimming gold medallist? Was it Eddy Merckx, the five-time winner of the Tour de France? Or was it Frank Shorter, the Olympic marathon gold medallist?

They decided there and then that the fittest was surely the person who could do all three events back-to-back. With the argument decided, it was agreed to stage a competition, which Collins immediately termed the Ironman. The distances decided upon came from three separate sporting events held annually on the Hawaiian island of Oahu: the 2.4-mile Waikiki ocean swim, the 112-mile Oahu annual bike race and the Honolulu 26.2-mile marathon run.

Thus, within two years, an event that was spawned in a bar room argument had received big interest in the US, especially in California. It spread across the country, with short- to medium-distance triathlons fast becoming the norm. The big Granddaddy of them all – the Hawaii Ironman – was reserved for the purists, the super fit or simply mad hatters. At least that was the way it looked to most mere mortals in these formative years.

And so Justin Nelson had found a replacement for *The Superstars*, which was losing popularity. He sold the idea to the heads of RTÉ, and with that decided to cover the first-ever RTÉ All-Ireland Triathlon in 1983. It would be screened as a one-hour documentary. The distances had to be challenging enough to make it a true test of endurance fitness and interesting enough for a television audience, so that the viewer could respect the athletic feat and watch the footage in awe and admiration. Some observers would probably slam it as utter crazy and say it was a fad that would not survive, but that was bound to happen.

The winner of this first All-Ireland Triathlon would go to the remote exotic island of Hawaii, way off in the Pacific Ocean, to pit himself against the world's best – followed by RTÉ camera personnel plus the famous voices of RTÉ Sport, Jimmy McGee and Brendan O'Reilly, to shoot this once-off documentary for Irish viewing. It would be the perfect mix of sport and entertainment amid a paradisical backdrop.

Michael Walsh from Dublin was a good amateur international cyclist, and took the honour of winning the inaugural All-Ireland Triathlon, which was staged in Greystones in Co. Wicklow in 1983. He then travelled to Hawaii where he faced the unprecedented challenge of lining up for the 2.4-mile swim, 112-mile bike ride and 26.2-mile marathon run – all in temperatures of over 90°F. The distances of the All-Ireland Triathlon had been half the full Ironman distance, and thus became known as a Half Ironman. Yet Walsh battled through the event to finish 276th out of 1,450 starters. In the process, he made history in becoming the first Irishman to compete in and, indeed, finish the Hawaii Ironman. These days, over 1,800 athletes qualify out of 30,000 hopefuls to do the Hawaii Ironman.

I strongly suspect I was the first Irish person to participate in a triathlon when I took part – and actually won – the Contraband Triathlon in Lake Charles, Louisiana, US on May 22, 1981. What I am sure of is that I was the first Irishman to have won a triathlon in the US.

What is also true is that I won the inaugural All-Ireland Triathlon in Sligo in 1984, and on the back of that success founded Limerick Triathlon Club in October of that year, the first triathlon club in the Republic of Ireland. Eight months later, I also started the Kilkee Triathlon – better known as the "Hell of the West" – which is the longest running triathlon in Ireland and still one of the best. Kilkee, a seaside resort, is where my family own a summer house and where I holidayed each year from the age of three. When I established them, I had no idea how long the Limerick Triathlon Club or the Kilkee Triathlon would last.

Seven All-Ireland Triathlon titles and five wins in the Kilkee Triathlon, along with representing Ireland in European and international triathlon and Ironman events, helped establish me as one of the fittest endurance athletes in Ireland in the period 1984 to 1991. Then, on the day of that freak accident in August 1991, my life as the best triathlete in Ireland was history. Someone else would have to earn the title and fly the flag for Ireland on the world triathlon stage. At the time, all I could do was struggle to survive and find a new identity.

Triathlon is truly a universally participated-in sport. It is a lifestyle for so many people and, of course, a very healthy one at that. Limerick Triathlon Club has also grown from strength to strength, with over 300 members now, and the Kilkee Triathlon is so popular that places are sold out within hours of it being announced each year. Some 140 triathlons were staged in Ireland in 2011, with participation of over 15,000 – and of all ages, genders and ability.

When serving as club chairman from 1984 to 1990, I designed the original Limerick Triathlon Club logo. Using a tenpenny piece, I drew three interlocking circles, akin to the five Olympic rings, placing a swimmer in the first, a cyclist in the middle and a runner in the third, which in my mind represented the new sport involving three events, yet making up one new sport – triathlon.

It is satisfying to look back in time and realise that the hard work, the time and input was worth the effort, not just on a personal level, but more importantly in leaving a legacy whereby many people can continue to enjoy and engage in this healthiest of pursuits.

After helping to pioneer the sport of triathlon in Ireland, I then returned to the US to pursue a profession in physical therapy and thus handed over my responsibility as chairman of Limerick Triathlon Club. At this juncture, the club committee nominated and appointed me Lifetime Honouree President of the club, and presented me with a black blazer with the club logo on its crest. The blazer is too tight a fit now but is proudly displayed as part of the Hartmann Collection, a small sports museum in the University Arena at the University of Limerick, which has several hundred items of unique sporting memorabilia.

Limerick is known as Ireland's sporting city. Indeed, it was a designated European City of Sport for 2011. As a true Limerick man, born and bred in the city, I am proud of my roots and of the many sporting and professional achievements in my fifty years of existence. My name through my work is universally linked to the success I have had as a physical therapist, working with many of the stars of world sport. What I now understand is that being a consummate professional – spearheading developments and methodologies in treating musculoskeletal injuries in the elite sportsperson, and being willing to do anything to address the process of healing injuries – is what I replaced my previous passion for triathlon with. It has made me not only proud of my contribution to triathlon but proud of how it shaped me.

I still get great satisfaction when I see how popular the sport of triathlon has become: it is now a valued member of the Olympic family. I was the physical therapist to the British Olympic team in Sydney 2000 and witnessed first hand the inaugural Olympic Triathlon. That was spectacular.

Many years later, standing on the promenade in Puerto del Carmen watching a group of swimmers training, it feels like only yesterday that I was training with unbridled enthusiasm in preparation for an upcoming triathlon. What seems to me to be only yesterday was in fact twenty years ago.

The 11-and-a-half-stone, super-fit champion of Irish triathlon is now a 50-year-old, 14-and-a-half-stone recreational weekend warrior – and as I have aged and changed so too have the sport of triathlon and, indeed, the Ironman.

One thing is still true: triathlon and Ironman had taught me well. I took the same missionary zeal that I had in becoming a champion in triathlon and simply transferred it, with all my energy, into my career as a physical therapist.

Whatever passion, hard work, discipline, focus and drive I had to reach the top in triathlon, it took that and more to reach the top in my career as a physical therapist. My experience proves that if one has the qualities to succeed in one endeavour in life, there is no reason why success isn't possible in another. Whether you get knocked down in sport, in business or in health, with a positive attitude and by tapping into the same qualities that made you successful in the first place, you can be successful again.

3

My Decision to Pursue Triathlon

In the spring of 1981, two years before the first All-Ireland triathlon took place in Ireland, I was on the second year of a four-year athletic scholarship at McNeese State University in Lake Charles, Louisiana. I had left Ireland in 1979 full of hope and promise to make it as a runner.

The oppressive heat and humidity of the Deep South was a limiting factor, but also the man with the stopwatch – my coach 'Bullet' Bob Hayes – wasn't exactly developing my potential either. My running performances were going down hill fast under his tutelage. Ironically, I did not know the story of this infamous coach until I had left the university.

There was already something of an Irish trail to McNeese State University. Fanahan McSweeney from Fermoy was Ireland's sprint record holder and also worked for Aer Lingus as an 18-year-old in Shannon Airport. He later competed in the 1972 Munich Olympics over 400 metres and desperately wanted to avail of expert coaching in the US. RTÉ sports commentator Brendan O'Reilly, who would cover my exploits in Ironman and World Triathlon Championship events, and was himself an Irish champion high jumper in his younger days, encountered Fanahan McSweeney on one of his journeys to the US, when he was embarking at Shannon. O'Reilly promised McSweeney that he would make enquiries about the best coach for an aspiring Olympic sprinter. The rest, as they say, is history.

O'Reilly landed McSweeney a four-year scholarship to McNeese State University, believing he would be coached by Bob Hayes, the Olympic champion in the 100 metres at the 1964 Tokyo Olympic Games.

On the first day of track practice, McSweeney enquired about when he would meet Coach Hayes, expecting to see the muscular black sprinter who was the fastest man in the world. With that, a skinny white man with spindly knees replied, "I am Coach Hayes."

Anyway, McSweeney survived at McNeese, but after two years I had enough and applied for a transfer to the University of Arkansas to train under the famous coach John McDonnell. The plan was also to team up there with my good friend Frank O'Mara from Limerick and fellow Irishmen Paul Donovan, Dave Taylor, Ronnie Carroll and Tommy Moloney.

American National Collegiate Athletic Association (NCAA) rules meant I was ineligible to compete for one year. When competing under NCAA rules, it was also forbidden to compete in open road races, at least where prize money was on offer. I had no such issue as I was finished with McNeese State University, so I entered the Contraband 5-mile road race in Lake Charles and won easily enough in 24 minutes and 5 seconds.

Upon receiving the winner's trophy, the Mayor of Lake Charles congratulated me and asked if I was participating in the other two events, which were designed to make up the first-ever triathlon event in Louisiana.

I had never heard of a triathlon. But, delighted with my win, I was eager to know about it. The format for those competing was, first, the 5-mile road race, which I had just won, and a couple of hours later, at the Convention Centre, a quarter-mile swim in a 25-yard pool, followed at 3.00 p.m. by a 15-mile bike race along Lake Shore Drive. The person with the lowest aggregate time would be the winner.

I just about survived the swim and then won the cycling race, to my surprise. With that, I not only discovered a talent on two wheels, but I won my first-ever triathlon competition in what was the first-ever triathlon event staged in the State of Louisiana. In the process, I suspect I became the first Irishman to participate in a triathlon.

It all made for one crazy day in the Deep South. Indeed, had a college mate not been kind enough to drive me back to the university six miles away to borrow an eight-speed racing bike, I would never have sampled the triathlon experience as a still naive 21-year-old.

The celebrations were in Louisiana Cajun fashion – an outdoor feast of crawfish, jambalaya and lashings of Coors beer. I was as sick as a mad dog afterwards for three full days. A day to be remembered and forgotten all at once, and yet the biggest problem to come out of it was how to get the four-foot triathlon winner's trophy home to Ireland. If my memory serves me well, I gave it to the college mate who had helped me source the bike, as I reasoned no one in Ireland would appreciate me winning a run, swim and bike race in Lake Charles, Louisiana. They'd probably think I made the whole thing up.

Back in Ireland a year later, and a year before RTÉ held the first-ever All-Ireland Triathlon, a young chap by the name of Tom Heaney, from Newtownards in Northern Ireland, won a triathlon. That was September 1982, and the event that Heaney won in Craigavon is now recognised as the first triathlon held in Ireland. It consisted of a six-mile run, a half-mile swim, a nine-mile cycle, another half-mile swim and then a two-mile cycle. Like my Louisiana Triathlon experience in 1981, a triathlon in those formative years was more of a try-athlon than a three-event competition – swimming, biking and running in quick succession.

Heaney was an international swimming champion. He was three years younger than me, and, although he had been in triathlon from the very start, his star would be six years in the making before he too became an Irish triathlete of international standard. When he was at peak shape in 1987, he beat me fair and square.

By 1983, after studying Business Administration for four years in the US, I had moved back to Limerick. I was a young 22-year-old, still eager to pursue my running career while also working full time in my family's 120-year-old, fourth generation jewellery business at 2 Patrick Street in the heart of Limerick City.

There weren't many people in the early 1980s who were full-time runners or professional sportspeople. People worked five days per week, from 9.00 a.m. to 6.00 p.m., and any sport was fitted in around that.

After a couple of months back in Limerick living with my family, it was obvious to my parents and my three sisters that I was on a different timetable. Each morning I was up and out at 6.30 a.m. for a six-to-ten-mile morning run, and at 6.30 p.m. I trained again with Neil Cusack, a winner of the Boston and Dublin marathons, often racking upwards of 120 miles of running in a week.

I remember my dad took me aside one day and sat me down for a serious talking to: "You have had your four years in America. You must put the running aside and knuckle down to taking work seriously." Little did he or I know about the bug that was about to take me by storm.

In February 1984 a chance viewing of the 1983 Hawaii Ironman on RTÉ stimulated my interest to enter the 1984 All-Ireland Triathlon to be held on June 17 in Sligo. To this day I don't know how my mother feels about her decision to rush out to the back shed to where I was feeding the dog and say, "Gerard, come in, there is a sports programme on TV which I think you would be interested in watching."

I was interested alright; absolutely absorbed by it, in fact, and the lights did not go off in my head that night. I had found what I wanted to do. I just needed to buy a bike and get cracking on the training to be ready in four months' time for the challenge. Whatever about fitting running in twice a day before and after full days at work, I was now faced with training for three disciplines.

I trained with the mantra, "The more you do the better you get." It involved getting out for a ten-mile run or two-hour bike ride at 6.00 a.m., to be back home for breakfast at 8.15 a.m. – a big double bowlful of Alpen to fuel the day – then a quick shower and straight back out to open the jewellery shop at 9.00 a.m.

The shop closed for lunch from 1.00 p.m. to 2.00 p.m., and most days I'd lock up the shop, jump on to the bike and tear up the city to St Enda's Sports Complex to squeeze in a one-mile swim. Then I'd rush back down to Patrick Street to make it back just as Cannock's Clock struck 2.00 p.m.

On occasion, I would do a few extra lengths of the pool to find I was running behind time, and, when I pulled up outside 2 Patrick Street, staff and customers would often be waiting for me to jump off my racing bike to open up the shop for afternoon business.

At 6.00 p.m. it was gear on and straight out the door for a two-hour cycle, followed by a six-mile run out by the river bank, arriving home by 9.00 p.m. for a meal covered in tinfoil, which my mother had made up and laid out for her now triathlon-focused son.

Travelling to Sligo for the All-Ireland Triathlon entailed a five-hour bus journey, with stops in every town en route. Yet my journey was nearly over before it began when the bus driver at Colbert Station refused to take my bike on board. A brainwave took hold of me. I dashed over to the train station to where I knew a fellow Limerick Athletic Club athlete, Freddie McInerney, was working. Freddie saw my distress, and whatever he said to the bus driver did the trick. My machine and I were Sligo bound.

The following morning, I woke up in Sligo with no doubt that I was ready to win the big race. My training had been meticulous, but now I had to check the course. In one of the wettest days I can recall, I cycled the 56-mile route and the following day, the day before the triathlon, I cycled the 6 miles out to Rosses Point from the Sligo Park Hotel to do a one-mile swim, leaving my racing bike hidden in the long grass on the rough of Sligo Golf Club grounds. That evening, I ran the 13.1-mile course to ensure I knew what was facing me the following day.

At 7.30 a.m. on the morning of the race, I was first into the dining hall for a gigantic meal to fuel up. After a few minutes, an elegant well-dressed man with a vaguely familiar face looked at me lashing and scoffing my face with food. It was Ronnie Delany. At the time, Ronnie Delany was the chairman of Cospóir, the Irish Sporting Organisation, and he had travelled to Sligo as a guest of honour to start the race and to present the awards. He asked me if I was in Sligo as a participant or spectator of the triathlon. I told him that not alone was I competing, but I was confident I would win the event. He smiled and wished me good luck.

When I did win the event and later met Ronnie again, he exclaimed that he had not expected me to finish the event, never mind win it. When he had seen all I had eaten for breakfast, he was sure it was the perfect recipe for an all-day stitch, or worse.

The 1983 winner Michael Walsh was gunning for his second national title, and he exited the swim ahead of me and powered his way around the cycle route. He had the experience and miles in his legs from long, tough days competing in the Rás Tailteann. I had to run like hell to catch him. Walsh had six minutes up on me as I started to run out of the Sligo racecourse.

I remember Brendan O'Reilly of RTÉ shouting out, "You are six minutes down. Do you think you can make it up?" On camera my response was captured: "You bet I can. I'm going to win this thing."

Running at five minutes and ten seconds per mile, against Walsh's seven minutes per mile, I soon passed him just after the four-mile mark. I had gobbled him up – and I already felt like the admiral of the fleet, heading for the first of many wins. Running the half marathon in 74 minutes saw me cross the finish line down by Sligo's Garavogue River in 3 hours 57 minutes, with second place finisher Adrian Byrne, another cycling specialist from Dublin, coming in 10 minutes behind.

The faces of RTÉ commentators Brendan O'Reilly and Thelma Mansfield went into shock when they attempted to interview me. I ran through the finish line, straight over to the pier, took off my running shoes and sports top, and jumped into the river. You see, instead of wishing during the last miles of the run for an ice cold drink, I had visualised crossing the finish line and basking in the cold flowing river. I floated in the river for ten minutes. RTÉ's camera crew in the helicopter above captured the moment.

Ground camera crew, Justin Nelson, Brendan O'Reilly, Thelma Mansfield and a large crowd had deserted the finish line 100 metres away to watch and wait on the shoreline to see the new All-Ireland Triathlon champion. The interview was conducted and I was driven away to the Sligo Park Hotel, where a banquet dinner and awards were handed out that night. I never got to greet any of the athletes who finished behind me at the finish line.

On that day in Sligo in June 1984, RTÉ was not the only media organisation covering the event. The international magazine *Triathlete* had sent its feature writer from the US and the Irish Triathlon was given a five-page feature, with the photo of me crossing the finish line making centre spread. The new sport was catching on very quickly. Ireland also had its own triathlon magazine, *Triathlon Ireland*, edited by Edward Smith from Belfast, who went on to become a sports producer with BBC Northern Ireland. The *Irish Runner* magazine, edited by Frank Greally, also gave triathlon generous coverage in the early years, and Frank and Lindie Naughton of the *Evening Herald* also travelled to Sligo to pen articles on the race.

Then came something of a bombshell: after my first All-Ireland Triathlon win, RTÉ announced that the all-expenses-paid trip for the winners was not to Hawaii for the Ironman, but to Nice, in the Cote d'Azur, France, for the Triathlon World Championships.

Hawaii would be a far more attractive proposition for any true triathletes. The Ironman was the ultimate. It was the Mount Everest of the sport. I had watched the TV episodes of *Hawaii Five-O*, and felt I already knew Hawaii. But this time Hawaii would have to wait. The head honchos up in Donnybrook were taking the cheap option, I reasoned. Although, actually, this was not the case: by the mid-1980s the Ironman was truly established as the ultimate in endurance events, but triathlon, as a sport outside of Hawaii, was also establishing itself as a very capable and attractive sport. Indeed, the Nice Triathlon, organised by the Mark McCormack International Management Group and funded by the Ville de Nice, had a far better prize fund for the top-twenty professional athletes. Nice was vying for having the world's best triathletes competing in its event, which consisted of a 2-mile swim, a 77-mile cycle and a 20-mile run.

Triathlon had earned its stripes. People were now very clear that an Ironman competition meant a 2.4-mile swim, a 112-mile bike and a 26.2-mile run, and triathlon itself was any swim–bike–run competition under those distances. From a commercial perspective, triathlon was suddenly very hot. Bicycle companies wanted to be associated with top triathletes using their product. Running shoe companies and swim attire companies likewise.

The big steel Peugeot bike that I rode to win the All-Ireland Triathlon was like a rusty gate by international standards. Kieran McQuaid, brother of Pat McQuaid, now the president of Union Cycliste Internationale, and his business partner Shay O'Hanlon, a four-time winner of the Rás Tailteann, came to my aid. They operated President Cycles, a bicycle distribution company, and they kindly supplied me with state-of-the-art Vitus aluminium bikes and decorated the frames with President Cycles stickers. The Vitus frame was the exact same machine that Seán Kelly rode with the KAS Team, the professional Spanish-based team of which he was lead cyclist. It was super light-weight compared to my steel bike, which I still kept as a workhorse for winter riding. I had made my first rookie mistake. The new bike was top notch, but, in taking delivery of it days before travelling to Nice, it had not registered with me that it would take time to get accustomed to the new machine. Nice was not going to be so nice after all.

The 1984 Triathlon World Championship was a watershed for RTÉ, for me and also for the women's winner of the Irish championship, Diane Sloan from Belfast. The cycle course in Nice was a 77-mile route that ventured into the Maritime Alps, and up steep climbs and narrow roads with treacherous descents. Diane Sloan, Michael Walsh, Adrian Byrne, Dave O'Connor and I trained on the course a few days before the big event. On a tricky descent, Diane crashed into an oncoming car and hit the windscreen full-on. She had a choice: to pull hard left and hit the car or avoid the car and go over the cliff parapet, with the potential of falling down almost 500 feet to likely death. She broke her leg in several places, and that ended her involvement in the sport of triathlon. But she still raised a smile the following day.

This meant that, on race day, RTÉ only had its male Irish Triathlon champion to focus on. Fortunately, a group of Irish triathletes who finished in the minor placings in Sligo were given £500 each by RTÉ towards the trip to Nice; so, Adrian Byrne, Michael Walsh, Dave O'Connor, Ann Kearney and Donia Nugent also travelled and, in some ways, saved the day.

Some 35 miles into the cycle event, in my first season doing triathlon as Ireland's flag bearer in the Triathlon World Championship, I crashed head-first into a wall after breaking too late trying to negotiate a hairpin bend. The bend had come all too suddenly, and so too did the wall.

In complete shock, and still driven by adrenalin, I remounted the bike with my front wheel buckled and forks bent. I managed about a mile, weaving from side to side with fellow triathletes passing me and staring in disbelief at this crazy bloodied Irishman still riding on, like a drunkard trying to stay upright. I was oblivious that my bike and I were both badly banged up. I was soon lifted off the bike by two gendarmes and placed in the back of an ambulance. The tone of a siren of a French ambulance is a sound that still haunts my ears to this day.

I was rushed to the famous St Roch Hospital in Nice. The journey down the twisty mountain took an eternity. Sixteen stitches to my head, a broken collarbone and concussion were the end products of inexperience and applying the brakes too hard. If I had to take a driving test for cycling a bike on a straight road I would have passed, but I would have failed a test on a twisty road outright. At the time of the accident I was in 36th position and moving swiftly through the field, only for the accident to strike. Perhaps I was too young and too driven by adrenalin to make it a successful day.

My mother Thecla waited among the crowds at the finish line on the Ruhl Plage, on the Promenade des Anglais, for her son to finish. Sirens blared, everyone babbled in French, German or Italian. She knew something was amiss when I did not come across the finish line in the top twenty. She strained her eyes to see into the distance and each athlete looked like her son until they loomed closer. Panic bells started ringing. She enquired. Nobody knew. Eventually she was told that I, "Dossard 254", had an accident and was hospitalised in the nearby St Roch Hospital. I was in pain and badly beaten up when my mother visited.

Later that night she met the winner of the race, Mark Allen of the US. He would go on to win a record seven Nice Triathlon World Championship titles and six Hawaii Ironman titles. The following day, Mark Allen visited me in the hospital and gave me a good luck card. He encouraged me to stick with the sport. That meant so much from one of the greats of triathlon.

The next day, Justin Nelson and Brendan O'Reilly and a dozen or so of the Irish competitors and their friends visited as well. RTÉ did not have much to cheer about. They went back to Dublin empty handed. Maybe Hawaii was a better option after all.

After three days in St Roch Hospital, I flew into Dublin Airport assisted by my mother. Instead of going straight home to Limerick, it was arranged to admit me to the Bon Secours Hospital in Glasnevin, Dublin to undergo a full medical with a CT scan, followed by a period of medical supervision because of the head injury. It was while in the hospital in Dublin, looking out a window each day for a week, that I decided to give triathlon a real go.

Regardless of the setback I had in Nice, irrespective of what my parents thought of this demanding and dangerous sport their son was involved in, neither they nor I had control over where it was taking me.

I was gripped by the triathlon bug. I came to learn years later that it's not only athletes at the top of the sport who train day in and day out to reach peak shape, but the triathlon bug is a worldwide phenomenon. People from all walks of life, and of varying ages and abilities, get hooked on triathlon as a lifestyle and many get so gripped by it that it controls their lives; they become so obsessive that it is all they live for. In extreme cases, some allow the triathlon to upset the balance between family, work and other important aspects of their lives.

4

The 1985 All-Ireland Triathlon and My Ticket to the Hawaii Ironman

After a full week in the Bon Secours Hospital, I was home in Limerick with my arm in a sling for five weeks, under medical orders not to do any training for eight weeks. With plenty of time to kill, I started formulating training plans for the following year. I was thinking big: the plan was to defend my All-Ireland Triathlon title, and to compete with the very best in the business at the European Championship and World Championship events.

When I made my decision in the hospital that I was going to give triathlon a real go, a few things were clear to me: I had raw athletic talent but my swimming was a big weakness, and I was a danger to myself and others on the bike. I would have to learn quickly how to swim and cycle if I was to be a force internationally in this demanding sport. But I had a problem: in 1984 there was no 50-metre pool in Ireland.

In Limerick, there was St Enda's Sports Complex – now sadly closed – and Roxboro swimming pool, which is now also gone. These were the two swimming pools open to the public in the city. But there was another problem: there was no lane swimming. The Masters Swimming Club was not yet in existence. The elite Limerick Swim Squad, headed by Gerry Ryan and Mick Mulcair, trained at St Enda's each weekday from 6.00 a.m. to 8.00 a.m., but that was reserved for the serious competitive swimmers.

It was only in 1986 that it became possible for me to join in their training. I had to earn my stripes and gain some proficiency in swimming before being welcomed into their close-knit fraternity, where the average age of the young competitive swimmer was 14 and I was then a 24-year-old runner turned triathlete, with no formal swimming background.

The public open hours at St Enda's were a quagmire. Rather than swimming, people stood or walked about the shallow end. Those who swam did a width from side to side, and then stood by the poolside for minutes before attempting to cross over again. The only reasonable time to go, when the pool was not jammed full, was from 10.00 p.m. to 11.00 p.m., for what was termed "adult hour".

The truth was, in the 1980s, very few people, with the exception of competitive swimmers, could swim properly in Ireland. A visit to a swimming pool was more of a social occasion, a good place for a chit-chat and dip followed by a scrub in the hot shower. To see a good swimmer glide up and down the pool was rare.

With no organised swimming, my strategy each night was to get in the pool, keep the head down and belt up and down like there was no tomorrow, trying to avoid crashing into people and just dealing with the random black eye, bloody lip or kick in the ribs encountered when a far larger man doing the breaststroke kicked a foot into me.

In those early days I surely caused some consternation, with my main target being to cover 80 to 90 lengths of the 25-metre pool – a mile and a quarter to a mile and a half – in the 50 minutes before the "get out" whistle was blown at 10 minutes to the hour.

Being eager to squeeze in another few laps, I always pretended that I didn't hear the whistle, and Paul Earls, the pool attendant, would have to tap me on the head to clear me out, sometimes being angry with me, other times giving me a big grin.

My swimming practice in 1984, and most of my training for triathlon, was more about survival, but at the same time it was ideal practice for the start of the swimming event in the World Championships or Hawaii Ironman, when 1,800 people charge into the water at the same time, all heading in the same direction. Imagine 1,800 people charging in and churning the water, jostling and fighting for space, two arms and two legs swinging, adrenalin pumping, all go at a frantic rate. Nowadays, with the exception of the Hawaii Ironman, events are begun in wave starts, with a limited number of people allowed in each.

Peter Snow was the manager of St Enda's Sports Complex in 1984. I badly needed him on my side. I met with Peter and repeatedly petitioned him to assist in making structured swimming training a reality. I requested a lane to be roped off for distance swimming. Peter agreed, but there was a catch. His dilemma was that most people paying to come in to use the pool could not swim a full length, with many not being confident to swim in the deep end. They mainly loitered in the shallow end and attempted widths. If Peter put down a rope for me and a couple of hardy triathletes then he would have been cutting off his nose to spite himself, as the 50 to 60 recreational users would not have been very impressed – and that was putting it mildly.

In the end he agreed to rope off one lane, the one furthest to the left, and he placed a sign poolside stating, "Reserved for Distance Swimming".

The one catch which I had to work around was that this rope was only down during the hour 10.00 p.m. to 11.00 p.m. It was a start, and beggars can't be choosers. But it meant putting lights on my bicycle and cycling the three miles there and back in the darkness. At least on the very wet or wintry nights my dad would drive me up, and after a few trips he ended up getting into the pool himself and swimming a few lengths.

The other step in my triathlon plan was to join Limerick Cycling Club. Top Limerick cyclist Gearóid Costelloe, who won a stage of the Rás Tailteann in Tralee in 1984, introduced me to many of the intricacies of cycling: how to glue a tubular tyre, or a tub, as they are called, onto the wheel; how to distribute body weight when cornering; how to use the breaks so you won't go flying over the handlebars; pedalling technique; and bike set-up and position on the machine. It was all new to me, but I couldn't learn fast enough.

Arthur Caball, who owned the Burgerland fast-food restaurant in Limerick's William Street, was a sports fanatic. He had followed my exploits, coming from nowhere to win my first All-Ireland Triathlon. Arthur met me one evening and outlined a proposition that I found hard to refuse. He wanted to sponsor me £4,000 in assistance, and all I had to do was to endorse and wear the logo of Burgerland on my competition sportswear. I arrived home excited. But my parents were having none of it. There was no way their son would be paid to wear "Burgerland" on his kit.

It was my loss, as they say, and Limerick Cycling Club's gain. I mentioned it to Gearóid Costelloe. His eyes lit up. The club could badly do with some funding and new team jerseys. Arthur agreed to meet me with Gearóid. A deal was struck, and with that Limerick Cycling Club had a sponsor. The club was delighted, and I was voted in at the club's AGM as press officer of Burgerland Limerick Cycling Club, with a special agreement that I myself did not have to wear the Burgerland logo.

Besides, I had my own ideas. I wanted to form a triathlon club. At this stage there were a couple of clubs in Northern Ireland, but none down south in the Republic. The sport was still so new, still in its very infancy. At the time there was no training manual, no book on triathlon, no coach with triathlon knowledge. It was an era of discovery, mostly by trial and error. As a champion of the sport, people looked to me for direction. I had spent four years on an athletic scholarship in the US, and I had come home and gone straight out and won the National Triathlon by some considerable distance. Everyone looked to me for the answers, but the fact was I didn't have any particular knowledge, just a bigger engine. But that's not to say I didn't learn fast.

I asked Peter Snow if I could use one of the offices at St Enda's Sports Complex to hold a meeting. I wanted to form Limerick Triathlon Club and help establish an identity for the new sport I was already mastering. I hand drew a couple of posters announcing a meeting and inviting anyone interested in triathlon to attend, and put them on the noticeboards of St Enda's Sports Complex and Roxboro swimming pool. With that, Limerick Triathlon Club was formed on 25 October 1984 and the five people who attended are credited with being founding members of the club. We were, in no particular order: Gerard Hartmann, Peter Snow, Yvonne Snow, Tom O'Donnell and Albert le Gear. All we really got on the night was a show of hands, but at least it was a start and Limerick Triathlon Club was born.

That November of 1984 Justin Nelson's RTÉ coverage of the All-Ireland Triathlon received a top viewership, partly due to it being well advertised in the *RTÉ Guide* but also due to the fact that there were only two channels in Ireland at the time: RTÉ 1 and RTÉ 2. So 8.00

p.m. on a dark winter's night, with the GAA All-Irelands won and lost, was an ideal time to show a sports programme, especially when there wasn't much of an exciting alternative on RTÉ 1.

By June 1985, Limerick Triathlon Club membership had grown to about 50 people. Throughout Ireland, other clubs formed – in Cork, Galway, Sligo and Westport, and several in Dublin. For the true fitness fanatic, the next challenge and logical step up from the marathon was the All-Ireland Triathlon in Sligo.

It was no coincidence that the All-Ireland Triathlon in Sligo was a success. Pat Curley, the race organiser, was a dynamic individual with great vision and enthusiasm. At his core, he too was a true sporting fanatic, and a person who got things organised and done in his stride. In his own sporting days he was a formidable sprinter, and, along with being a physical education teacher in Sligo's Summerhill College, he coached and was a positive influence on many of Ireland's best athletes, including Irish 1,500-metre and mile record holder Ray Flynn, as well as international 800-metre runner Roddy Gaynor.

Pat was a dynamo who put his heart and soul into organising the All-Ireland Triathlon in Sligo. With the help of his right-hand men, Tom Staunton and Aidan Anderson, and a hard-working organising committee, it was assured success from the start.

Pat had also been a local councillor and was highly respected in Sligo. Through his vision and connections he had the backing of the community, local governing bodies, the Town Council, the County Councils of Sligo and Leitrim, the Sligo Yacht Club, Sligo Golf Club, the local police, ambulance and medical back-up, plus the Civil Defence. Then, with RTÉ covering the event, it would get maximum exposure.

Pat Curley's vision was to put Sligo on the global sporting map. Where better in the world to host a televised triathlon than in Yeats Country, with Ben Bulben and Knocknarea as spectacular backdrops?

Rosses Point Beach was a perfect location for the 1.2-mile swim, and the scenic country roads around Sligo town and county were safe and ideal for a Half Ironman event. The 13.1-mile run had athletes run the length of Rosses Point Beach onto the Sligo Golf Club, across two fairways and onto third-class roads, before meeting the main Sligo–Bundoran Road running into Sligo, and then running the five miles out to the finish line on the wide promenade of Rosses Point, where thousands of spectators waited for the finishing athletes, while being entertained by music and race updates.

Unlike now, when there are some 140 triathlons of all distances in the country, the majority being the short sprint distances, in Ireland in the 1980s triathlon meant one thing and one thing only – the All-Ireland Triathlon in Sligo or the "Sligo Tri", as some people called it.

For the 1985 event Pat Curley upped the ante and invited several international top-rated triathletes to Sligo to make it a battle royal at the elite level and give it some international exposure. Nico Mul, from the Netherlands, had finished eleventh in the 1984 Hawaii Ironman, and we were told he ate rusty nails for breakfast. Mul did indeed turn up – he was going to put me to the test. The event sponsors, Premier Dairies and Puma, in alliance with RTÉ and Pat Curley's triathlon committee, made it worthwhile for him and a couple of foreigners to compete, and enticed them further with a first-place prize of £750. The stakes were high, as I had a title to defend, but RTÉ had confirmed that the men's and women's Irish champion would receive an all-expenses-paid trip to compete in the Hawaii Ironman that October. That was all the incentive I needed.

Another visitor blew in overnight to almost spoil the day. News from the meteorological office the day before that All-Ireland Triathlon, set for Sunday, June 23, 1985, warned of severe gale forces and inclement weather. Hurricane Charlie had blown up a storm of mass destruction along the south-eastern coast of the US, and also caused massive damage along the Gulf Coast.

Pat Curley and his organising committee woke up to their worst nightmare. Perhaps they should have had a plan in place, in case of a storm or emergency, to stage the race on an alternative day. But RTÉ cameras and crew were on hand; somehow the show had to go on. At 9.00 a.m., when I arrived at Rosses Point to set up my bike and gear for a big performance, it all looked very ominous. The starter's gun was set for 10.30 a.m.

Over by the car park at Rosses Point, everyone had clambered into a large rusty corrugated shed that had "Triathlon" painted on its roof. I met Pat Curley and he greeted me with his usual positive attitude: "Gerard, my man, don't worry, we're going to start on time."

There was confusion everywhere; people were shaking their heads. It was still gale force eight, with thirty minutes to go, when Pat Curley's voice came on the PA system. Normally he would be heard loud and clear, but with the wind howling and rain lashing only a few heard his message. The sea looked rough and ugly. This was going to test the nerves and rumble the stomach. It was decided to cut the length of the swim from 1.2 miles to just short of a mile.

So the 1985 All-Ireland Triathlon began with a huge dash into the incoming waves. Within minutes, a dozen or more competitors had pulled out, abandoning the triathlon they had trained months for. Spectators on the beach watched the drama unfold, with support canoes bobbing up and down and often out of sight in the stormy waters. At the time, wetsuits were a luxury not yet invented for triathletes, although "rusty nails" Dutch champion Nico Mul was wearing the top half of a surfing suit. On such an inclement day almost all the participants exited the sea shivering; some were taken away by the medics to be treated for hypothermia.

Despite all the drama, most of the starters, with the exception of those who elected to bail out early, made it safely back to the shore. I came out of the water in eighth place, and took my time to change into full biking attire. Where was Mul? I didn't know.

It was just a matter of survival for the first twenty minutes on the bike. I was shivering and my teeth were chattering uncontrollably, and most of my energy went into simply holding onto the handlebars and battling against the wind that seemed to hit from all angles. Out on the Bundoran Road, the helicopter with RTÉ cameramen overhead, it was signalled to me that the leaders of the race were about a quarter of a mile ahead and I was closing in. In the lead were Tom Heaney and John Glass, both from the North. After I powered past them, with 30 miles to go, all I had was the lead timing vehicle in front of me to concentrate my mind.

I visualised the car as a competitor leading the race and I kept pushing on, not knowing who behind me was playing catch-up or how the day would unfold, except that I had no intention of relinquishing my title. The day that had begun so bleakly began to brighten up just as I started the run. When I got to the far end of Rosses Point Beach, I took one good look backwards and there was nobody in sight. I had a lead of at least the length of the beach, so I settled into my customary pace – five minutes, twenty seconds per mile. With five miles to go, I was just entering Sligo town and the run out to the finish at Rosses Point, when I saw my dad standing beside his car at the side of the road waving his hands and shouting: "Slow down, slow down, there's no need to rush!"

Running the half marathon course in 73 minutes ensured that I had won the triathlon in 4 hours, 4 minutes and 30 seconds, a massive 14 minutes ahead of Adrian Byrne who had been the runner-up the previous year. In third place was Drumbo's Desi McHenry – better known as Superman, as he sported Superman-like Lycra attire. Nico Mul finished fourth, and claimed afterwards that he never warmed up. Ann Kearney from Dublin was a revelation. Ann, a 36-year-old house-wife who trained three times each day and won all the mini-triathlons in the run-up to Sligo, had exited the sea earlier in the day a shivering and forlorn figure, so frozen she could hardly walk up the beach. She thawed out and stuck in for a long day, finishing third behind new women's champion Juliet Smith from Malahide, whose winning time was 5 hours, 5 minutes and 30 seconds, and Donia Nugent from Galway, the Irish record holder at 24-hour and 100-mile ultra running distance events, and truly one of the toughest women in Irish sport.

It was a rough day all round, but I had won my ticket to Hawaii to compete against the best in the world in the most famous triathlon of them all – the Hawaii Ironman.

5

Ironman –
The Ultimate Test of Endurance

Getting to participate in the Hawaii Ironman was one of the most exciting episodes in my career as an athlete and has had a positive influence on my life outside of sport. Above all, it taught me that the impossible is possible.

Imagine it's February 18, 1978 and you are one of fifteen supposedly brave people standing on San Souci Beach in Waikiki, Hawaii. You are looking out into the sea, casting your eyes 2.4 miles across to where your bicycle is waiting. The waves are rolling in and your stomach is in a knot. What have you signed up for? Are you stone mad?

After completing the swim, and in the event of no shark attacks, you will mount your bicycle and ride 112 miles around the island of Oahu in the midday sun – when perhaps only mad dogs and Irishmen would venture out. After finishing the mammoth bike ride, ideally unscathed, you then run the Honolulu Marathon course, a full 26.2 miles. If you finish all that, then you're an Ironman.

As it turned out, only twelve of those fifteen brave souls finished the first Ironman in 1978. Each received a trophy, handmade by its founder Captain John Collins, of a metal Ironman with a hole in its head. The same trophies were not to be awarded again until 2003, when each finisher of the 25th Anniversary Hawaii Ironman Triathlon, myself included, received a replica of the original trophy upon crossing the finish line, with the inscription "Swim 2.4 miles, cycle 112 miles, run 26.2 miles. Brag for the rest of your life."

> You vow,
> You curse
> And you chant,
> I'm done.
> No Way.
> Never again.
> Then the crowds,
> The lights,
> The Medal.
> The pain is all forgotten.
> And you hope you'll get the chance
> To do it all over again.[1]

Gordon Haller won that first-ever Ironman, in a time of 11 hours, 46 minutes and 40 seconds, ahead of John Dunbar, who finished in 12 hours, 20 minutes and 27 seconds, and Dave Orlowski, who came in third at 13 hours, 59 minutes and 13 seconds. These first Ironmen were true explorers, pioneers of something they had no idea was going to explode and some day become a global phenomenon.

In 1985, at the age of 23, I did my first Hawaii Ironman. Like those first pioneers, I stood on the shoreline not knowing what to expect. I looked out over the ocean into the far distant horizon with excitement, fear and trepidation, praying to God that this day would go well, that I would survive and live another day. At the start line, in the water among 1,800 brave souls, you either stand or tread water, waiting for the blast of the cannon to sound the start.

> You are surrounded
> Yet so alone,
> Alone to plan and dream,
> To hope and pray
> The day to come
> Will have it all,
> The highest highs

---

[1] *from* Bob Babbitt, *25 Years of Ironman Triathlon World Championship*, Oxford: Meyer and Meyer UK Ltd, 2004.

And the lowest lows.
The fact that it is hard
Is what makes it special;
It's also what makes it IRONMAN.[2]

I was about to enter new territory in every sense. The Hawaii Ironman is different to any other test of endurance. It is swimming, biking and running large distances with a backdrop of intense heat, raging winds on the bike course and a marathon course with no shade.

Ironman was growing so fast that when I completed the event in 1985, and crossed the finish line in ten hours and four minutes – over one hour and forty minutes faster than Gordon Haller's winning time eight years earlier – twenty-three athletes had finished ahead of me. Nowadays, the thousands of enthusiastic Ironman triathletes and sold-out events worldwide indicate that what had started as a casual event among friends was actually the birth of a movement, and I am forever grateful that I was part of those early days. I experienced the Hawaii Ironman in an age when participants carried all their needs for the day on the bike ride, as if going on a picnic, as the aid stations served only bananas, quarter oranges, peanut butter sandwiches and a sports drink that was either plain water or de-fizzed Coke.

The Ironman is an event that changes people's lives, no question about that. There is something very special about attempting the near impossible. Obviously a lot of people see it all as plain crazy, and yet humans love a challenge: climb Mount Everest, run a marathon, swim the English Channel, do the Hawaii Ironman. The Hawaii Ironman is not so easily doable anymore, however. Ironman qualifying events are held on all continents, with over 30,000 people vying for the 1,800 starting places in Kona, on Hawaii's Big Island, every October. The dream of every triathlete is to do an Ironman, and the ultimate dream is to compete at the biggest party of them all in Hawaii. Crossing the finish line in Hawaii makes one a member of an exclusive club. It is a club where the dues are perseverance, dedication and a will to finish, and all that can test the toughest nut.

The mantra in Hawaii is: "To finish is to win and to win is to finish." The natural forces on the island of Hawaii make it a challenge nobody

---

[2] Babbitt, *25 Years of Ironman Triathlon World Championship.*

can take for granted. In other triathlons and Ironman events, the top professionals have their race strategy and timing down to a science. In Hawaii that goes out the window. The best in the world have, at one time or another, been reduced to the brink of collapse, to walking the marathon. To change strategy is the secret, and being able to revert to plan B is almost a must.

Most top athletes will finish in daylight before the sun sinks into the Pacific Ocean at 6.00 p.m., but a puncture or two out on the bike course, a stitch in the stomach, or a pulled muscle or leg cramp can leave the fittest struggling to finish. When the course marshal hands them the glow-in-the-dark neck band, their day continues. Instead of finishing in the top echelon, they are happy to be able to shuffle along, because the sight of the floodlit finish line on Ali'i Drive, with the thousands of spectators and supporters, is all that matters on Ironman day. Whether it is a run, a shuffle or crawl across the finish line, for any triathlete it means one thing: confirmation that the impossible is possible and the cheer from event announcer Mike Reilly: "You are an Ironman!"

To finish is to win, to win is to finish – only those who have crossed an Ironman finish line understand this completely. When you finish the Hawaii Ironman, you carry something deep inside yourself that you can call on whenever you need to. When life gets tough, you can cope with and handle whatever has been dished out, whatever bad deck of cards has been thrown your way, because you have completed the toughest day in sport. It is a badge you wear inwardly, proof of an inner power and self-belief that you can call on forever.

The Ironman has become my lifelong teacher. It teaches how to plan, how to efficiently manage time, how to have a balanced life – in terms of juggling family, work and training – if there is such a thing for an athlete. It teaches how to deal with adversity. Nothing else will teach you as much in one day about yourself as a day in the Ironman in Hawaii. You might have all the training done and bought the fanciest and fastest bike that money can buy, yet at that starting line you are all alone. Then, out in the lava fields, some 50 or so miles from Kona, with the trade winds blowing with all their might and the sun melting you to a frazzle, you find yourself pushing along on black tarmac so hot an egg would fry on it. At this point you may have to dig into your soul and ask a lot of questions of yourself. You find out who you really are. Curve balls are thrown at you to test your mettle as the endless road ahead shimmers into the horizon. And you still have a marathon to survive, with no guarantee that you will ever see the finish line.

To this day, I draw on the Ironman as my source of inspiration. When life gets hard, when it all goes wrong, when I face a day that is a struggle from the start, when people put demands on me that are unrealistic, when a flight is cancelled and I get stuck in an airport for a day, I stay strong. I draw on Ironman, knowing no matter what happens I can handle it. Ironman Hawaii has taught me well. I wear the badge and I will take it to the grave.

6

A Sponsorship Controversy

After winning my second successive All-Ireland Triathlon in Sligo, I was on a high. I took the following day off, my first rest day in six months. Even the day before the race, I ran for one hour in the morning, swam for one mile and cycled for one hour in the evening.

There were only eighteen weeks to the Hawaii Ironman and, while I was only one full year training and competing in triathlon, I had no fears of the challenges ahead. I had never cycled further than 60 miles, yet now 112 miles was my challenge. I had never raced a full marathon, and in four months' time I would face a marathon in a furnace of heat that I had never experienced, not even in the heartland of the US when I was a student.

I contacted Con O'Callaghan, the president of the Irish Triathlon Association. Con was very politically involved in the development of the sport in Europe and he served as the inaugural chairman of the European Triathlon Union (ETU). He was a sport administrator and recreational triathlete, based at the House of Sport in Upper Malone Road, Belfast. Triathlon was growing fast, and was particularly strong in Germany, France, the Netherlands and Britain, and there was a lot of political wrangling in those days, with the powerhouse of the sport, the US, pulling the sport in one direction and the ETU also fighting its cause.

This was all very important on a larger scale, because the sport of triathlon was like a ship on rough water. It needed stability and Con O'Callaghan worked tirelessly in those early years to steady the ship. If triathlon was ever to be a mainstream global sport it needed to have its own world governing body, and it would be another four years before the International Triathlon Union (ITU) staged its first international distance World Championships – in Avignon, France in 1989 – and fifteen years before triathlon became an Olympic sport, at the Sydney Olympics in 2000.

My only request to Con was to enquire if the Irish Triathlon Association could fund my way to any international events, in preparation for Hawaii. Perhaps, as a young 23-year-old, I was naive. The Hawaii Ironman was a financially lucrative event, and the most successful triathlon of them all, but Con O'Callaghan had no interest in the bit players. It did not concern him if I needed high quality races to improve my standard. He was a sports administrator and just another politician within the sport. I was on my own regarding preparing for Hawaii.

The European Championship Triathlon took place in Denmark on September 1, a few weeks before I was scheduled to travel to Hawaii. First, with the Ironman coming up, I had to arrange to take time off work for another event and then there was the concern of how I would fund the trip, and, indeed, how I would get there. Fellow Limerick Triathlon Club man Michael Carroll from Roscrea, whose best placing in the All-Ireland Triathlon was tenth, agreed to drive me to Denmark in his old Renault. The logistics of it were far from ideal. First, fitting two road bikes into the car was a challenge. Then came the drive to Dublin for a boat from Dublin to Holyhead, followed by an eight-hour drive to Harwick, where we boarded the boat for a twenty-hour trip to Esbjerg in Denmark, to arrive in Aabenraa after another two hours in the car.

Arriving in Aabenraa the day before the race, hardly able to walk with a stiff back, Michael and I jumped into the sea – only to get out as quickly as possible as we were both stung all over by large jellyfish.

The following day, I faced the European Triathlon Championships in a subdued mood, knowing that straight after finishing we would have the long haul back home, where, with no rest, I would return to work. I was deflated, exhausted and too drained to gallop. This was before the race.

In any case, in my first European Championship Triathlon I crossed the finish line in twelfth place overall, three minutes outside the bronze medal, wondering what the result would have been had the funding and support structure been in place for me to fly from Shannon. At the awards ceremony after the race, Con O'Callaghan approached me and said, "Not a bad effort."

I walked away shaking my head, knowing that he had no interest in helping me reach the top of triathlon internationally. My best Half Ironman time of three hours and fifty-seven minutes would have won me that European title by four minutes, but there could be no regrets as it was all part of participating in a sport in its infancy.

Nonetheless, if Ireland was to have a presence on the world stage and get its top performers on victory podiums in international competitions, serious structures would have to be put in place. The approach of those governing the sport would have to change. Sometimes such people get confused and use their positions of power to self-serve and help their own climb up the political ladder. The administrators and sports governing bodies are there to govern and run the sport, and serve the elite athletes. They must always put the athlete first and facilitate them performing at the highest level. Many administrators have it backwards, and play the big and mighty, treating the athletes like dirt as if the athletes should be at their beck and call.

Working at several World Championships and the past five Olympic Games as a backroom staff member, I always put the athlete first. They need to be given every opportunity plus the platform and support to enable them to perform at their best.

When I travelled with teams in the early 1990s, the administrators and medical staff often got priority seating and accommodation, and this infuriated me. As an athlete, I saw firsthand how athletes were treated and I had a good yardstick when I travelled to international competitions and shared notes with athletes from other countries. The "blazer brigade", as I called them – the officials and administrators on junkets for their own gain – are thankfully in the minority nowadays, as sport on the international stage has become such big business. It is highly competitive and results are what count.

After the European Triathlon Championships in Denmark, I was interviewed for a feature article in the 1985 *Triathlon Ireland Annual* magazine, and my quotes at that time summed up my sentiment:

My experience in Denmark showed me that an Irish triathlete striving to reach the top is only bashing his head against a brick wall in comparison to the opportunities afforded to my counterparts on the continent. I was amazed to hear a Swedish competitor who finished six places behind me say that he was a full-time triathlete who spends upwards of seven hours training daily and belongs to a heavily sponsored team along with [getting] support from the national triathlon federation. My feeling from Denmark was that the standard will continue to rise and unless Ireland's top performers are given some assistance in terms of sponsorship or financial assistance then our standard in top competition will drop even lower.

In ways, nothing changed for many years, and the ongoing dilemma for some athletes is the same now as it was then. Athletes need most support on their way to the top. Once he or she has reached the top ten in the world in his or her chosen sport, the Government steps in and gives out the maximum funding of €40,000 per year – but the athlete who reaches that level already has commercial sponsorship deals, and prize money to boot. It is at the stage when the athlete shows potential, and is on the way up, that finance and coaching and medical support are most critical.

In my seven years as Irish triathlon champion, I never had any input from the Irish Triathlon Association. The association worked on an administrative level only, and it felt to me as if the athletes were inconsequential, mere bit players. That was most unfortunate as there was so much potential. In the 1980s, Ireland had international-level potential in Ann Kearney, Tom Heaney, Noel Munnis, Kevin Morgan, Erwin Cameron, Eamonn McConvey and Eugene Galbraith – all very accomplished athletes, but they had to fend for themselves.

The net result in any sport where there is no performance structure in place is that top results do not happen. World-class high-performance sport in the 21st century is now an intensive, exhausting occupation where athletes are fully embroiled in sophisticated training regimes, utilising scientifically developed technologies that create long-term physiological and personality changes, as they progress through the higher levels of the sport to the ultimate prize of an Olympic gold medal. Lord Sebastian Coe, a double Olympic 1,500-metre champion and one of the finest sports administrators around, is a man I greatly admire. I meet him on occasion through my work, and I always listen intently to what he has to say. He has his finger on the pulse. When the Great Britain Olympic Team, of which I was a backroom member, had a hugely successful Olympics in Beijing in 2008, Coe stated:

> What we have witnessed here is the amalgam of good administration within governing bodies, world-class coaching, elevated levels of funding and hungry and motivated competitors. If you bring these four things all together you tend to get people up on the rostrum. It is very important that we now recognise that there is no happy accident out there in the sports arena.

I had learned a big lesson in Denmark. Never again was I going to travel halfway around the world to arrive so tired that a day in bed was all I was able for, not a championship event.

Hawaii was indeed more than halfway around the world. When I looked for it on the world atlas it took me ages to find it: there it was, way off from the west coast of America, a speck of small dots. It was going to be another long journey to get there, maybe an Ironman journey in itself, even before the big event.

I was keen to know what the actual deal was going to be in terms of the "all expenses paid" trip to Hawaii. I reasoned that, to be able to do justice and represent Ireland in this toughest of events, I should get out to Hawaii at least two weeks before the race, to get over jet lag and the nine-hour time difference, plus to acclimatise to the heat and humidity. Everyone I spoke to agreed: "Wouldn't that be nice, two full weeks in paradise?"

What they didn't realise was that I was effectively going to jump into the sea and swim two and a half miles, jump on my bike and cycle from Limerick to Dublin, and run the Dublin City Marathon – all on the hottest summer's day you've ever seen in Ireland, plus another twenty degrees. An all-expenses-paid trip to Hawaii back in 1985 was the ultimate trip and a free ride for some, but not for me.

I contacted Justin Nelson in RTÉ: "Justin, Gerard Hartmann here. Yes, the training is going great. I'm just phoning to find out what date has been organised for travelling to Hawaii?"

The Hawaii Ironman was scheduled for Saturday, October 26. I came off the phone scratching my head and totally confused. The plan was for me and the Irish contingent of seven athletes to depart from

Dublin Airport on Tuesday, October 22, with the RTÉ personnel of Justin Nelson, Brendan O'Reilly and camera crew. The planned itinerary would involve almost two days of travel to get to this speck of an island on the Thursday, two days before the race.

I was fuming. Denmark and the Half Ironman weeks earlier did not seem too bad after all. I phoned my good friend in Sligo, Pat Curley. Pat completely understood my plight and put in a few phone calls for me, but they fell on deaf ears. The budget for the RTÉ programme televising the 1985 Hawaii Ironman had been decided and there was apparently no room for manoeuvre.

I put pen to paper and wrote to the Irish event sponsors Premier Dairies and their head man Frank Nolan. Premier Dairies had pumped over £20,000 into the Sligo All-Ireland Triathlon, as they were its key sponsors along with Puma. The requirement was that every competitor in the All-Ireland Triathlon had to wear a competition shirt emblazoned with a large Premier Dairies logo on the front and a smaller Puma logo. Premier Dairies agreed to sponsor us for the Ironman and the deal would be the same as for the triathlon: the Irish competitors would wear the gear provided and live by the mantra "He who pays the piper calls the tune."

That was fine, but I was the star athlete. Nice, the previous year, had been a watershed, when I had ended up in hospital because of an accident. So, this time I risked my trip and made it clear to them that I would not compete in Hawaii unless a reasonable deal was struck to fund me to go to Hawaii two weeks beforehand. I had no reply to the letter I sent to Frank Nolan at Premier Dairies or the copy of it I'd sent on to RTÉ. I'd kept a photocopy, so I sat down and put pen to paper again and sent off the two letters as if the previous had never been sent, only this time registering both. I reasoned that if these boys were messing with me, while I was breaking my arse training three and four times per day, then they were fooling no one. After a couple of weeks waiting for a reply, I phoned Frank Nolan and explained that if Premier Dairies did not fully fund my trip to Hawaii on the earlier date that I requested, I would seek additional sponsorship myself to fund it. Their loss was going to be someone else's gain, and there would be red faces galore for all the wrong reasons.

I knew John O'Donnell, one of the stalwarts of Limerick Athletic Club, who worked for many years with Guinness. John had qualified for the 1948 Olympic Games as a sprinter but missed out due to administrative issues. He knew firsthand how vital it was to travel early and acclimatise. John made an appointment for me to meet Guinness's head of marketing PJ McAlister.

PJ and I struck a deal: Guinness would fund me £2,000 and in return I would wear the Guinness logo on my competition kit. It did not matter that, back then − and to this day − I was one of the few Irishmen who had never even tasted Guinness, never mind drank a full pint of the black stuff. What ructions would develop did not become apparent until a couple of days before the race in Hawaii.

After what happened in Nice the year before, my mother was not going to let her 23-year-old son travel to the remote island of Hawaii on his own. The day before travelling, I cycled from Limerick to Kilkee in Clare and back, a full 112 miles – the same distance I was going to cycle in Hawaii, though of course I knew the experiences would be worlds apart. Cycling for five and a half hours on a wet September day in the west of Ireland bore no similarity to cycling 112 miles in temperatures close to 100°F across lava fields on a wind-swept paradise island. After getting off the bike in Limerick, I then ran thirteen miles. I came home, had a good feed and spent another hour taking the bike apart and packing it safely into a big box padded with Styrofoam that had been kindly made for me by a factory in Askeaton, without charge.

The following morning my mother and I flew from Shannon to New York and on to Minneapolis, where we had to stop over for the night. Next stop the following day was Los Angeles Airport. Looking out the window of the airport, my thoughts went back to the previous summer and the Los Angeles Olympics, and I thought that if John Treacy could win a silver medal in the heat of California I should be able to survive the heat of Hawaii. The flight from mainland US to Hawaii was all of five hours, almost the same distance as from Shannon to New York. "Lord," I remember thinking, "these Hawaii Islands really are in the middle of the ocean, actually the most remote group of islands in the whole world."

When we stopped at Honolulu Airport we had a three-hour wait before boarding our next flight to the Big Island. I was jumping out of my skin and eager to get out for a run. I had my running shoes on and I had a singlet and shorts in my hand luggage – ever the athlete, always ready for a run. I changed in the toilets and went out squinting into the glaring midday sun, as I had not even thought of the need for sunglasses. Before even starting to run, I was soaked in sweat. The heat was like a furnace as I ran laps of a car park at the airport in the 95°F heat for some 45 minutes.

We arrived in Kona Airport in darkness and waited at the luggage carousel for our luggage to arrive. With the little airport deserted, we realised we had arrived empty handed, with the exception of small carry-on bags. We were told that our luggage and my bike had to be re-routed and would probably arrive in the next day or so. Whatever about plans to get out and train on the course, at least I had my running shoes and sweaty gear – fortunately so, as the bike and luggage took four days to arrive. We were given $300 by the airline to purchase some clothes and necessities, and of course the first thing I did was buy a pair of swimming goggles and togs so I could get swimming in the warm Pacific.

It was utter paradise. A swim in the pristine clear sea every morning at 7.00 a.m., followed by a breakfast of jumbo pancakes with maple syrup, and mango and papaya so fresh and tasty it made my mouth water for hours. Training and acclimatisation were going well, almost too well, I suspected. On the Saturday, a week before the race, I swam for an hour in the morning, covering most of the swim route, and straight after I ran 21 miles in 2 hours and 10 minutes. Later in the day, I cycled a hard 40 miles, averaging 23 miles per hour.

The following morning, neither my mother nor I were fit to get out of bed. We both woke up with the same symptoms: bad headache, feeling very hot then very cold, weak legs and sore throat. Walking from the bed to the bathroom was an effort. We were jinxed. We both spent four days in bed, and when my sister Leonie arrived from Dublin days before the event, hoping to have a few relaxing days on a paradise island with her mother and brother, she found us isolated and quarantined in our hotel bedroom; we could only speak to her on the phone.

On Thursday, October 24, two days before the race, I woke up feeling better and I went out and jogged three miles. The RTÉ crew and group of athletes had arrived in from Ireland. I met with Justin Nelson and Brendan O'Reilly, and I explained my plight. I had been sick and did not know if I had the energy to participate. Brendan O'Reilly sat me down and explained to me that in 1956 he had made the high jump qualifying height, three times in fact, for the Olympic Games in Melbourne. He was on an athletic scholarship at the University of Michigan, and each day he waited for a letter or telegraph to arrive from Ireland, notifying him that he was going to the Olympic Games. When eventually the telegraph did arrive, it read: "Trip cancelled; insufficient funds".

Brendan had sadness in his voice when he told me his story. His Olympic chance was scuppered by the blazer brigade, who probably sent a couple of officials too many to Melbourne instead of its qualified Irish champion high jumper. Brendan explained that he would never forgive their meanness. He explained to me that the ultimate in sport is to compete for your country in the Olympic Games, representing your people. He expanded by saying: "When you are young it seems like you will stay forever young, and that there will be many opportunities to participate in the Olympics, and the reality is that an opportunity may only knock on the door once, if ever." He encouraged me to at least start the Ironman, to be part of a very special day, to grab the opportunity and do my best.

I always found comfort in speaking to Brendan. His was the voice of RTÉ Sport that I had grown up hearing. He was a gentle giant of a man, who in essence was a fellow athlete. He, too, had dreams and opportunities taken from him. I had worked too hard for this day and an untimely bug was not going to rob me of my chance to participate in my first-ever Hawaii Ironman World Triathlon Championship.

I registered for the race and went through the customary regime of having to hand in the competition clothing in numbered bags. Cycling gear, helmet and shoes were put in one bag to be collected and handed out upon exiting the swim. Running shoes and the necessary singlet and shorts were put in another bag to be handed to its rightful owner once he or she came into the bike-to-run transition zone. I discovered the organisation behind the Ironman to be awesome. It takes 7,000 volunteers to support the Ironman, to make it all work like clockwork, so that 1,800 finely tuned athletes can have their day in the sun, in every sense.

My gear was registered, and I would not see it until after the swim and again after the bike ride – if, indeed, I got that far. I had a couple of green t-shirts printed with my sponsors' names on the front: Guinness's logo on the top and Premier Dairies' logo underneath. The morning before the race, Justin Nelson phoned my room wanting to come by with his film crew and Brendan O'Reilly to conduct a pre-event interview with me. When I arrived for the interview, the first person who greeted me was Premier Dairies Marketing Manager Frank Nolan. Frank went as white as a sheet when he saw me. There I was, standing in front of him with a big Guinness logo on my shirt and his branding underneath it. The truth of the matter was that he had not played ball or offered to negotiate any middle ground with me. He who pays the piper calls the tune, perhaps, but it was taking two sponsors to pay this piper's expenses – not because I was mercenary and trying to make money out of the occasion, but because I wanted to compete at the top level, which meant getting to Hawaii a couple of weeks in advance of the race to acclimatise and ensure I had a chance. I had my principles.

There was utter mayhem. Justin Nelson and Brendan O'Reilly came into the fray. When I sat down to talk to Frank, of course it made matters worse. As I sat, the Guinness logo was on display and the Premier Dairies logo was completely crumpled and hidden. There was a lot of bickering and barking and we were just short of throwing punches when I agreed to do the RTÉ interview wearing a polo shirt that Brendan O'Reilly took off his back. Little did Justin Nelson and Frank Nolan know that, earlier in the morning, I had done an interview for the US broadcaster NBC's *Wide World of Sport* wearing a green shirt with the Guinness logo. Nobody in the US would know who Premier Dairies were, but everyone knew Guinness – and Guinness certainly got value for their sponsorship buck.

The sports gear that I would wear in the race was checked in now, and Justin Nelson made an attempt to have me change to wearing cycle shorts and running gear that Premier Dairies had made up. But it was too late. When they didn't bother to respond to my registered letters,

On my First Communion day, 1969.

The 1979 All-Ireland Junior Steeplechase event. I am no. 28; my good friend Paul Moloney (of adidas fame) is no. 29. Standing to the extreme left of the photo is my friend Fr Frank Madden, who was tragically killed by lightning.

MARATHON RUN IN AID
OF TROCÁIRE.
Sunday April 1st. 1979.....
COPSEWOOD — LIMERICK — COPSEWOOD
25 MILES.

Total amount collected... £ 400.

Extract from my training notebook from 1979 about the school marathon run I did to raise money for Trocáire. Clockwise from left: the poster I drew up and stuck on the school notice board; with Fr Patrick Donnellan, head master, and Fr Joe Harrington, rector, Salesian College, Pallaskenry, Co. Limerick before my charity run; I ran the 25 miles in under 2 hours and 40 minutes, without once stopping or taking a drink of water; students cheer me on my way.

Me, Coach "Bullet" Bob Hayes and Fanahan McSweeney at McNeese State University, Louisiana, 1980. Fanahan competed at the 1972 Munich Olympics in the 400 metres for Ireland. After two years at McNeese, I had had enough and transferred to the University of Arkansas.

Five-Miler victor
Gerard Hartman is waved in by a race official after winnin the Five-Miler
(American Press photo by Randy Monceaux)

May 22, 1981: winning the contraband five-mile road race, which was the first of three events making up the inaugural triathlon staged in the State of Louisiana.

Start of the inaugural Sligo All-Ireland Triathlon, June 17, 1984. Hardy athletes brave the cold water; the luxury of using wetsuits in triathlon events did not come about until 1987.

HE ALL-IRELAND TRIATHLON

3:57:18
SEIKO

PREMIE

NE SLOAN, "THE GIRL FROM THE NORTH," AND GERARD HARTMANN OF LIMERICK WON TRIPS TO NICE

3:57:17
SEIKO TIMING

244

AZC 72

International magazine *Triathlete* centre spread photograph of me winning the first of seven All-Ireland Triathlon titles, June 17, 1984.

After my victory at the first All-Ireland Triathlon, June 17, 1984: RTÉ's Thelma Mansfield, me, RTÉ's Brendan O'Reilly and my mother, Thecla Hartmann.

"Double trouble" – with triathlete Diane Sloan from Belfast in Nice, France in 1984. Both Diane and I ended up in casts at the Triathlon World Championships in 1984.

Winning my second All-Ireland Triathlon in Sligo by a massive fifteen-minute margin, June 23, 1985.

Finishing my first Hawaii Ironman World Championship in 24th place, October 26, 1985.

Meeting Dave Scott, five-time Hawaii Ironman Champion from Davis, California, on Big Island, Hawaii in 1985.

Ironman swim start 1984. 1,800 brave souls charge into the Pacific Ocean to compete in the 2.4-mile swim, the first event of the Hawaii Ironman World Triathlon Championship.

Outside my family's fourth generation jewellery business at 2 Patrick Street, Limerick in 1986. At 25, sport was shaping my life and taking me in a new direction.

Being interviewed by RTÉ's Ronan Collins after winning the 1986 All-Ireland Triathlon at Rosses Point in Sligo. My mother, Thecla, who is standing between us, looks on.

Competing at the Triathlon World Championships in Nice, 1986. Above the city of Nice, the cycle route covers 77 miles and ventures into the Maritime Alps, up steep climbs on narrow roads with treacherous descents. The 1984 Triathlon World Championships had not been kind to me, but this time I was well prepared. I finished fourteenth overall.

The front of *Triathlon Ireland* magazine in 1987, depicting me running in the Triathlon World Championships in Nice. I ran the twenty-mile run in two hours and eight minutes.

Competing in the 1987 Japan International Triathlon. This was probably my best international finish. I had the fastest bike ride and the fastest run. I only finished third overall, as my swimming was my weak link.

Competing in the Hawaii Ironman, Oct 14, 1989. I'm out of the saddle, trying to make up time on the eleven mile climb to the half-way turnaround at Havi. I had one of the top cycling times – 4 hours and 48 minutes.

Winning the 1991 All-Ireland Triathlon at Rosses Point in Sligo. It would prove to be the last competitive triathlon I would have the physical capability to compete in at an elite level.

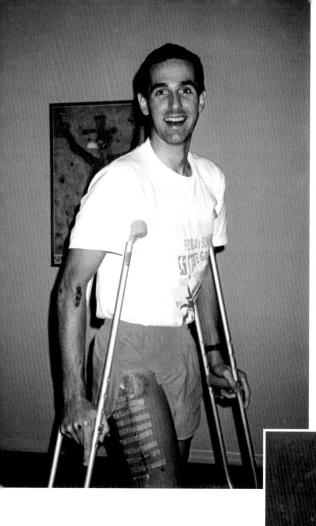

After the accident on August 28, 1991. For weeks, I was low and depressed, after breaking my hip and ending my career as an athlete. But I woke up one morning with a smile on my face and I have never looked back.

The end result of my accident is that I have enough metal in my right hip to set off alarms at security in airports.

Receiving the "Triathlete of the Decade" award in 1992 from Pat Curley, the founder and dynamo behind the All-Ireland Triathlon in Sligo.

In the Olympic Stadium at the Barcelona Olympic Games in 1992. It was my first Olympic Games and I worked with twelve medal winners. Nowhere else is the energy and excitement so electrifying as in a full Olympic Stadium.

With Sonia O'Sullivan at the Treaty Stone in Limerick City, 1995. Sonia is just after winning the World Championship 5,000 metres. I am very proud of my Limerick heritage and take great pride in bringing many of the world's sports stars to my native city.

At the 1995 RTÉ Sports Star of the Year Awards with friends Eamonn Coghlan, Seán Kelly and Jimmy McGee.

I was not going to give back an inch. Ironically, the sportswear that Premier Dairies printed with their logo was blue, white and red. The racing attire I wore was a green outfit, albeit with a logo endorsing the black pint with the white head.

7

"To Finish Is to Win and to Win Is to Finish" – Competing in My First Ironman

This account first appeared in the 1986 *Marathon Annual* magazine (vol. 1, no. 31):

A lava moonscape; 30–50 mph trade winds, 100-degree heat – the backdrop to the most famous triathlon of them all, the Ironman Triathlon World Championship. Two-time Irish Triathlon Champion Limerick man Ger Hartmann gives his own report.

By virtue of winning my second All-Ireland Triathlon in Sligo, I had won an all-expenses-paid trip to compete in the World Ironman Triathlon in Hawaii on 26 October 1985, compliments of sponsors Premier Dairies and Guinness. [...]

Throughout the summer I tackled my mission with great dedication. Training two and three and sometimes four times each day, on top of an eight-hour working day demands extraordinary willpower.

My goal was to finish in the top ten. Considering that the field of 1,800 athletes had already been narrowed down from 15,000 aspiring qualifiers, such a performance would demand superb fitness. Why so many people wanted to do this race, I was keen to find out. Most people wanting to do the race had to compete in select triathlons to qualify, [but] not me or the seven other Irish athletes participating in this, the eighth ever Hawaii Ironman: RTÉ had an agreement in place for the top placers in the All-Ireland Triathlon to automatically qualify.

In training for the race, I averaged weekly totals of 9 miles swimming (5 hours), 300 miles cycling (15–16 hours) and 60–70 miles running (7 hours), [a total] of 27 hours of training weekly.

Two and a half weeks prior to the event, I departed for Hawaii. My big concern was the climate. It was getting cold and the nights were closing in early in Ireland, so it was vital to have adequate time to adapt.

My first sight of the course was Ali'i Drive, which is where the swim starts and finishes at the pier, and where the famous finish line is situated. This is the nicest part of the course and the most sheltered from the sun, the only three-mile stretch in a total of 140 miles that has cover from the hot, energy-sapping sun.

On one side of the road you have Mauna Kea (a 14,000-foot volcano) and, on the other side, the aquamarine surf of the Pacific Ocean. Everywhere I looked tanned bodies were either running or cycling.

I was now to see the infamous cycling course. Prior to departing [for Hawaii], RTÉ executive sports producer Justin Nelson had warned me that the cycle route would be a mind-boggling experience. The road goes straight out 56 miles to the turnaround [at a tiny village named Hawi], and it is ramrod straight, with long deceptive rolling climbs […].

Its problem, which makes it famous and tests the nerves and every sinew in the body, is the simmering, sweltering, searing heat […] and winds – not the gentle breezes associated with palm trees in paradise island, but blustering tree bending gales that sweep over the desolate lava for hours […], which have knocked athletes from their bikes.

Heat, wind and the distance would have to be dealt with, but one week prior to the race I encountered my greatest obstacle. Dave Scott the six-time Hawaii Ironman winner stated: "Most people lose their concentration after about five hours when the mind gets delirious from the heat. It's not physical, it's mental. When you come to Hawaii it's like racing on the moon."

Before ever getting to the starting line, my problem was physical. I've never doubted myself mentally. […] Within a matter of an evening my mother, who had travelled with me, and I became suddenly ill. It hit us both like a storm that blew in, and it hit us hard. […] On my own I would have labelled this as heat stroke, but with my mother falling ill at the same time, and she had not exerted herself, it was obvious that it was a fever.

The following day, we phoned down to the hotel reception and requested a doctor to visit. The doctor called and examined us both and revealed that we both had a viral infection. There had been a viral epidemic on the islands in July and August, and it had not been fully eradicated. In a four-star hotel, he explained, you might have all the luxuries, but if the air-conditioning vents were not changed the virus would harbour in there and spread throughout the system from room to room, unknown to visitors. We were grounded […], stuck fourteen floors up, overlooking the swim course of the Ironman I had dreamt of competing in. I accepted more and more that I would not be able to compete.

Four days before the race, I ventured downstairs for a meal of pasta. I started to think, "Maybe it's possible." I tried an hour's cycle and still felt weak. The following day I went for a run and felt better. It was two days to the start. RTÉ's Brendan O'Reilly sat down with me and encouraged me to start. He reasoned, "Why not start?" I could see how it went and if I did not feel good I could always abandon [it].

My mind was set to be a part of a great day, regardless of whether it took me ten or eighteen hours to complete the course. Brendan assured me that to finish was to win.

At 5.00 a.m. on race morning I made my way to the check-in area.

Everywhere there was nervous energy. I made final adjustments to my bike, corrected my tyre pressure, put [on] water bottles and strapped three spare tyres to my bike in case of puncturing. One year in Hawaii, some fool tried to sabotage the race by putting down hundreds of nail tacks out on the road. A lot of cyclists pump their tyres up to 120 psi to find that, when the day heats up, the tyres expand with the extreme heat and [they] blow. I was well warned.

At 7.00 a.m., at the sounding of a cannon blast, I charged into the warm Pacific Ocean along with 1,600 other super-fitness freaks. The turbulence created by the swimmers clawing and churning their way through the relatively small area between the pier and shore was one experience I will never forget. The race starts on a small strip of beach aptly named Dig Me Beach. One hour and nine minutes later, I was back up on the pier, jostling through people to find my bike. Crowds cheered madly; the atmosphere was so electrifying that I had little time to ponder on how I felt. Minutes later, I was mounting my bike for the 112-mile journey into the moon-scape. […]

I was venturing into unknown territory. I had cycled 112 miles back in Ireland but I had never raced further than 56 miles, and now in the heat of Hawaii I was tackling double that.

As I left the Kona Pier, I viewed the first section of the [cycle] course. It was in my face – a near vertical hill extending for half a mile. At the top, the reward was a long stretch of highway surrounded by seemingly endless miles of black crusty lava. I bargained with myself to do every-thing but fall off into that field of lava. The desolate lava, barren of all vegetation except for occasional colourful bougainvillea, acted as an oven, baking the cyclists as the sun climbed in the sky. […] [The] temperature measured at the Kona Airport may give an accurate high of 92 degrees but the heat index, the heat out on the road that I was cycling on, the heat that my tyres were melting on, was over 115 degrees, too hot to walk barefoot on, certainly too hot to fall off the bike on.

Twenty-eight miles into the cycle, the RTÉ crew in their Toyota Jeep came up beside me and notified me that I had [been] placed 288th in the swim. My weakest event was over; now it was time to do some passing out, if my body could only stay strong. No one had passed me yet and as I passed dozens my confidence rose. I thanked God for the feed stations that came every five miles. At each opportunity I grabbed a bottle of water or de-fizzed Coke.

As I neared the turnaround point, I began counting the athletes ahead of me on their homeward journey. At 56 miles I was in 106th position and starting to feel strong. Everything went well until 90 miles into the cycle. I had hit the wall or "bonked", as the cyclist terms it. The strength in my legs, without warning, deserted me and when I looked down at my cycle computer I noticed that, instead of travelling at 22–23 miles per hour, I was helpless at 17 miles per hour. I was virtually crawling, and running out of gas. My training friend back home, Gearóid Costelloe, had warned me to expect the wall at around the 80–90-mile mark. He was spot on. The advice that he had given was not to panic because, unlike in running, one can go through the wall in cycling and come through and experience a second strength. His advice was a saviour. Sure enough, five miles later, after eating two bananas and [drinking] two Cokes, I felt strong again and was back stomping at the pedals travelling at 22 miles per hour, and faster.

Finishing the 112 miles, I saw the leading athletes starting out on their marathon. The first at this stage was eventual winner Scott Tinley, who had won the race in 1982 and had placed second in 1983 and 1984 to the great Dave Scott.

The runners looked well sunned and weather beaten, starting out with eyes sunken into their heads. In a few minutes I would be one of them and, with my best event to come, the chase was on. I was looking forward to getting off two wheels and legging it after them.

It was just 2.00 p.m. when I started my run and I had been pushing myself without stop since 7.00 a.m. I had never run a marathon before but I was eager to run through the field as high up as I could get. Running was my number-one sport and I had every intention of making my mark. From 88th place starting the run, I began counting the athletes as I passed them. At 10 miles my time was 65 minutes. The heat was at its highest and everything in the distance was just a mirage with the heat dancing off the tarmac. If you focused too far in the distance, the mind would go crazy. One step at a time, keep striding out; to jog or walk is to waste valuable time.

As I reached the turnaround, I met the lead runners on their way back. They all looked shattered, their faces drawn and glazed. I realised if I could keep my momentum going then maybe I would post the fastest run of the day. How many more could I pass as they fell off like dying flies? If I could just keep running, running all the way to the finish six miles away.

At twenty miles I still felt strong, still passed people like they were standing still. Could my fuel tank keep me going? At each fuel station I drank a cupful of de-fizzed Coke. Throughout the cycle I had consumed 14 bananas and a bag of figs, but on the run I dared not to eat in case I got a dreaded stitch. At 22 miles, my left leg started to tighten up. I was reduced to survival now. My catching-up-and-passing-out game was over for the day. I had four miles to go. I did not want to blow up now. To have to jog and walk to the finish would take an eternity. I am an athlete, a runner. I was suffering badly but I ran on.

The last two miles will live in my mind forever. The crowds were fantastic. "Go Ireland! Go Guinness! Do it for your country!" When you are that close to finishing your first Ironman, when the body is struggling but still willing, you don't care about your country; all that matters is getting to the finish line. The electrifying atmosphere carried me over the finish line. As I came up to the line, race announcer Mike Plant screamed out, "From Limerick the jeweller Gerard Hartmann. You are an Ironman!"

My time was ten hours and four minutes. I had run down all but 23 athletes to place 24th overall in my first Ironman. Under the circumstances, I was elated; four days earlier I was in bed and too sick to contemplate competing. After 140 miles of swimming, cycling and running, I joined the exclusive club of Hawaii Ironman finishers.

It had been a long, hard day. I had given 100 per cent and I will relish the experience and carry it with me for the rest of my life.

After every earthquake there is an aftershock. Weeks after returning from Hawaii, all hell broke loose. Behind the scenes of every sport there is politics going on, fuelled by people with issues and agendas. They say competitive sport is war without bullets. All the national newspapers had the story in their sports pages: "Row over Gear as Premier Dairies Pull Out." Frank Nolan put out a press release stating, "Premier Dairies do not wish to associate with a sport in which the leading participant operates to such behavioural standards."

I was infuriated, to put it mildly. Some executives with their big salaries were lapping it up in Hawaii on a junket, while I was pushing my body to its limit. I was having none of it. I put my response in writing: "I feel Premier Dairies are putting the full blame on me in an effort to hide their own inadequacy."

The Irish Triathlon Association set up a special three-man committee to investigate the situation. The *Irish Times* ran the story in December 1985, under the headline "Premier Pull Out":

A sponsorship worth £50,000 has been lost. The Irish Triathlon Association has set up a special three-man committee to investigate the row which blew up in Hawaii between Premier Dairies and the Irish Triathlon Champion Gerard Hartmann over the wearing of sponsor's gear. Premier Dairies, who reportedly pumped £50,000 into sponsoring the All-Ireland Triathlon and covering the Irish participants in the Hawaii Ironman event, have pulled out of any future sponsorship of triathlon because of the row which caused widespread disquiet.

In a hard-hitting letter, Premier's group marketing director Frank Nolan said his company would not sponsor the All-Ireland Triathlon in 1986 or future years. Nolan said the decision was entirely influenced by Gerard Hartmann's behaviour in seeking and accepting sponsorship for the Ironman in Hawaii from Guinness, in return for competing there in Guinness gear. "This," said Nolan, "was in conflict with the condition of his acceptance of our sponsorship of his travel, race entry fee and accommodation costs of participating in the Hawaii Ironman. We do not wish to associate with a sport [in] which the leading participant operates to such behavioural standards."

I travelled to Dublin to stand up for myself at the special investigation held in the Ashling Hotel. Frank Nolan had his turn ahead of me to tell his side of the story and it all seemed very plausible. That was until I got the opportunity to tell my story. From a young age, I have been extra meticulous in keeping diaries of all my training sessions and correspondence. I arrived well prepared, with photocopies of the letters I had sent to Frank Nolan at Premier Dairies requesting to travel to Hawaii earlier than the planned few days before the race. My letters showed very clearly that, in the event that Premier would not fund me to travel earlier, I would seek alternative sponsorship to facilitate that. Record keeping had saved the day.

My words alone would not have had the same impact as the hand-written evidence. Premier Dairies and Frank Nolan received a stiff rebuttal from the Irish Triathlon Association, who stood up for its leading competitor and stated: "This type of behaviour from a large organisation is unacceptable."

Still, the loss of the sponsorship was a blow. However, Pat Curley, the All-Ireland Triathlon organiser, was unfazed. RTÉ producer Justin Nelson once again committed to covering the 1986 Sligo event – so all was not lost. As it turned out, a new sponsor was announced within months, in the form of Sligo–Leitrim-based North Connacht Farmers Co-operative Society (NCF). Like Premier, NCF was a dairy business – and the 1986 event would be titled the NCF All-Ireland Triathlon.

The NCF sponsorship was actually a far better fit: it was a north-west business supporting the biggest sporting event in the north-west region. Their head of marketing Michael Hughes saw the potential of having me on board as a flag bearer for their dairy and meat products. He travelled to Limerick and we agreed a contract.

8

The Magic of Lasse Virén

Kilkee is a sleepy west Clare beach resort that comes alive every summer, and has served as a holiday retreat for many families, mostly Limerick people, for over 100 years. As I mentioned, ever since the age of three I have holidayed in Kilkee, and it has a special place in my heart.

My family own a home on the promenade, and on summer Saturday evenings in my triathlon training days, I would regularly lock up the jewellery shop on the dot of 5.30 p.m., gear up and ride out of Limerick on my road bike, head west past Ennis, on towards Kilrush – nearly always against the prevailing west wind – and arrive in Kilkee in two hours and forty minutes. Then I'd have a quick meal and bed down in preparation for my biggest training day of the week.

Getting up and out early on a Sunday morning in Kilkee is like waking up to a deserted village. At 7.00 a.m. the only semblance of activity is young people heading home from a hard night on the town. My normal routine had me in the water by 8.00 a.m. for my first of two one-mile swims that day. The second swim, after Mass, would be followed by lunch, and then it was time to gear up and cycle the 56 miles back to Limerick, 20 or so minutes faster than the cycle out with some assistance from the wind, to arrive at my home on the Ennis Road. Then I'd quickly change into running attire – as speedy as I'd have to be in a triathlon – and tackle an eleven-mile run back out the Ennis Road towards Cratloe and to the back gates of the Cratloe Forest. I'd touch the gate as a marker that I made it, record the split time on my Timex Triathlon watch, and keep the momentum going until I reached home, often clocking through 10 miles in 54 minutes and breaking the hour for 11 miles.

It was on one of my many swims in Kilkee Bay that I drummed up the idea of hosting a triathlon there. The Limerick Triathlon Club Committee agreed that it would serve as a great event, especially as we were to do it four or five weeks before the Sligo Triathlon. On a good summer's day in Kilkee, there is nowhere better in the world to be than participating in the Kilkee Triathlon, but on an inclement day, with west winds howling, just finishing the Hell of the West becomes a challenge in itself.

The race has been run every year by Limerick Triathlon Club since 1985, and starts and finishes in front of my family's summer home on the promenade, just beside the band stand. Every triathlete in Ireland wants to do the Kilkee Triathlon, with its 1,500-metre sea swim, 45-kilometre bike ride and 10-kilometre run.

I was fortunate to have won five Kilkee Triathlons in my prime, and when I think back on the success and enjoyment of that event, I am reminded that my involvement in sport very nearly didn't happen at all.

As a young boy, I was full of energy and always getting into trouble. I was tall and lanky, and had two left feet, as they say. I was cast aside in the school I attended as being a "messer", and too goofy and clumsy to be any good at sport. I hung around the school with fellow troublemakers, dragging on cigarette butts at the back of old prefab buildings. I was a real messer alright and needed an outlet for my energy.

One day I was called up to the front of the classroom for eating sweets during class. The teacher reached into his cassock and withdrew a long leather strap. I received four of the best on my right hand, four of the best on my left, four of the best across both knuckles and a full belt of the leather strap across both sides of my face. In total hostility I drew my right leg back. I was hardly able to kick a football but I propelled my leg forward and kicked with great force the front of the teacher's leg. I was immediately suspended, and I never set foot inside that school again.

It was in Kilkee in the summer of 1972 that I was saved from impending trouble. I was staying at the Strand Hotel with my parents and sister. My parents had their hands full to keep tabs on me. Every afternoon and evening, people crowded into a large function room to glue themselves to the television to watch the 1972 Olympic Games in Munich. As an eleven-year-old, I was hardly interested. I had never even heard of the Olympic Games. Olga Korbut of the USSR team was the star of gymnastics. The North American swimmer Mark Spitz was the sensation in the pool.

Then curiosity took hold of me when I witnessed the Russian sprinter Valeri Borzov win the 100 metres. A Northern Irish woman was also interviewed and she had won the Olympic gold in the pentathlon. The commentator was a young Brendan O'Reilly and the athlete being interviewed was Mary Peters. Over and over again, they showed the pentathlon competition in which Mary Peters had beaten her rival, the German Heidi Rosenthal. Then came Finnish athlete Lasse Virén, who tripped on the track with a Tunisian runner. He got up immediately, having lost twenty metres, but he just gave a quick glance to the lead runners ahead and bridged the gap within half a lap. That impressed me to no end. He was down but not out. He went on to win that 10,000 metres.

Just like that, I had found something to eat up my energy. My parents looked out the hotel window at their son and daughter playing Olympics on the beach. A line was drawn in the sand and I'd take off, sprinting like hell, and my sister would measure the performance. Barefoot, I'd run two lengths of the beach and sprint the last 50 metres, pretending I was Lasse Virén, and collapse into the sand. I did not need a coach or teacher to show me the way. I had found a sport myself that I could enjoy. Seven years later, the boy who was a "messer", who was too clumsy for sport, was bound for the US on a running scholarship to chase his dream.

I often wonder what would have happened if I had not witnessed those Olympic Games in 1972. One thing I could never have guessed back then was that my talents in another area would take me to several Olympics, working with the best athletes in the world.

What this experience shows is the importance of environmental conditioning, how it affects us both positively and negatively, and the importance of role models and encouragement. When I see TV programmes that are distasteful, violent and showing anti-social behaviour, I cannot but think of the negative impact that they can have on young children in particular.

I believe we are all born to be positive but conditioned to be negative. We all need encouragement and good role models. If we mix with people who are positive, cheerful, enthusiastic and expecting the best; if we are lucky to have parents and teachers who are supportive, encouraging and fair, then we have a good chance of being positive, cheerful and successful.

In my young life I was somehow conditioned to dislike school and to dislike sport. I had a bad experience at the hands of a teacher. Watching a small black-and-white TV in 1972 changed my life. Lasse Virén, Mary Peters and Valeri Borzov ignited a flame in me which still burns strong to this day. Being involved in sport gave purpose and meaning to my life. At the same time, it relieved a lot of pressure on my parents, as they really had no idea what to do with their hyperactive son.

Sport has shaped my life, has helped me to form values and has given me something very purposeful to do, and, indeed, dream for. One thing I am sure of is that every human being has been born with God-given talents. As an athlete, and now as a physical therapist, I feel blessed to have found my talents. At the same time, it frustrates me to see individuals with talents not using them or, worse still, squandering, abusing and disrespecting these talents. Everyday I am grateful for the talents and the opportunities that I have been given. These things can never be taken for granted – they give me reasons for appreciating them every day, but also to encourage youth, and people of all ages, to get involved in sport.

In 1979 I dreamed all year of winning one race in the All-Ireland Schools' Track and Field Championship. I had finished second the previous year, but I felt this was to be my victory year. I was beaten on the day by a very talented runner. He was a class act. Sometime later, at the 1986 World Triathlon Championships in Nice, he spotted me sitting in a restaurant. It had been seven years since we'd last met. He was overweight, and he explained to me his story – how he regretted not pursuing his athletic dreams.

In 1980 he was offered an athletic scholarship to the US, and, even though it was what he dreamed of doing, he instead went straight into his family business. It was obvious to me, sitting in the restaurant in Nice, that he was not happy.

A couple of years later, he took his own life. His sudden death shocked me. Here was a young man who had more athletic talent than me but did not follow his dream. I thought hard. I prayed hard. I made a pact with myself that I would use my talents to my best capability. I would always follow my star and do in life what was right for me.

Not long after this, I sadly witnessed the tragic death of one of my primary school friends. In fact, I saw him fall to his death from a window on the fifth floor of a building. I was standing twenty feet away when he impacted the street. The scene will live with me forever: looking up to where he had fallen from, the window wide open.

Moments later, a window three floors lower opened, and I saw his mother looking down at her son on the pavement. Within a minute, she was on the street covering her son's dead body with a blanket. To this day, a cold shiver goes down my spine when I recall that dreadful tragedy.

Sadly, of my 28 classmates from primary school, 3 ended their own lives. I have known nine men who have taken their lives. I think about them every day and wonder had they no hope, no vision or no purpose. Was their darkness so great they could see no light? Was the burden of life or self-imposed expectation too great? Were they not lucky enough to find their talents, their calling in life? I can only imagine the pain that they went through, and that of their families and friends. Suicide is a complex and perplexing subject, and is one that, unfortunately, is not going away.

I encourage people to follow their dreams, to go with their hearts. Invariably, if they do something that they love and are enthusiastic about, they are most likely to be successful and, more importantly, happy.

I think back on a poem I used to insert in my training diaries:

FOLLOW YOUR STAR

Follow your star
Whatever it is,
Don't be easily put down
By the pessimist's frown.

The goal that you set
In whatever line,
If you believe you can do it
Hope must never decline.

Though others may try
To push you aside;
Be steadfast, be resolute,
Go with confident stride.

To some measure of failure,
You may have to succumb.
No distress, no depression,
Success will soon come.

Your very own person
Resolve now to be,
And your Star you will reach,
Just try and you'll see.

(Maureen Sparling)

Now, more than ever, it is important to follow your star. The Celtic Tiger created havoc in people's lives. It created a false sense of being invincible. There was no reality. People took things for granted. The simple things in life lost meaning. It stormed in and people lost faith, direction, hope, and their values and ideals. Materialism ruled and the simple ways of life suffered. From reading the newspapers, anyone can see that the drink and drug culture has reached epidemic proportions, with many people using drugs to escape from pain and depression, and many more to make up for a lack of meaning and purpose in their lives.

I believe that sport and recreation are the ways forward. Everyone at some stage builds up frustration and anger – but whether it is triathlon, running, swimming, tennis, a game of five-a-side soccer, a bike ride or whatever sport, there is no better antidote, no better stress and anxiety reliever, than physical activity. It clears the mind, rids the body of unwanted stress and completely recharges the batteries.

9

The World Championships in Nice, 1986

Pat Curley was the master of drumming up interest in the Sligo All-Ireland Triathlon. He would phone me regularly and tell me how big the race was going to be this year and who he had coming in from abroad to challenge me for the title. He phoned me up in the first week of January 1986 to tell me that Tom Heaney, Noel Munnis and Eamon McConvey up North had given up their jobs and were training full time. He did not need to do a sales job on me – I was already wired and eager to win the three-in-a-row – but nonetheless his gamesmanship pressed my buttons further.

In April 1986, I received a written invitation to travel to Japan for the Japanese International Triathlon. The Japanese were famous for their fascination with marathon running and were now taking triathlon as seriously. They invited the top-30 finishers from both the Hawaii Ironman and the World Triathlon Championships from the previous season to their event on July 20, 1986. It was an honour to have been invited, but politics in sport intervened and showed its ugly side again. The policy was that the national federations were also informed of the invite. Thus, Gerard Hartmann, who had been placed 24th in the 1985 World Ironman Championships, received an invitation from Con O'Callaghan of the Irish Triathlon Association to compete in an international distance triathlon – a 1,500-metre swim, 40-kilometre cycle and 10-kilometre run – in Lurgan, Co. Armagh on May 17, along with the top 20 male triathletes and the top 10 female triathletes in Ireland, to determine who would go to Japan. I was 25 years old and working full time in my family's business earning £60 per week. I did not own a car and now I had to get myself to Belfast. My ever-reliable club mate Michael Carroll agreed to drive the forty miles from Roscrea to collect me in Limerick and take me on the five-hour journey to Belfast. The event was scheduled for the Saturday morning, with a 10.00 a.m. start at Lurgan Swimming Complex. We arrived late the night before and I put my bike together. I arrived at the start the following morning wearing a poker face, wanting to get the race started and won, and then to clear out of there as quickly as possible.

Tom Heaney, the Northern Irish star, was a Commonwealth swimmer and had been winning all the short races in the North. This was the Irish Triathlon Association's chance to put Hartmann up against Heaney, on his turf, and to try to give him a lever up to an international event. Tom Heaney, with his swimming proficiency, including the fancy tumble-turning, meant one thing only: he was going to make mincemeat of me in the swim and build up a huge five-minute advantage, which I surely could not make up.

Sure enough, Tom exited the swimming pool a full five minutes ahead of my poor swim performance. I pulled back two minutes on the bike and started the run three minutes behind him. Almost straightaway I was on his tail, and I caught him at the three-mile mark. With that, I kept the momentum and finished five minutes ahead. Michael Carroll put my bike in the car while I showered and we cleared out of the place as quickly as possible, just as we had planned.

Unfortunately, the Kilkee Triathlon was on the day I was due to fly from Shannon to Amsterdam for a long-haul flight to Narita Airport, Tokyo. But I could not miss Kilkee, so I took part and won the event by nine minutes, with my dad on standby to drive me to the airport. I had used my training bike in the race. We just about made the check-in. Had I thought too much about the logistics, I would never have chanced taking part; but, when you are young and eager, everything and anything is possible.

In Japan, the triathletes were treated with the utmost respect. All the athletes stayed in Tokyo for one night and the following day we were put in a five-star private carriage on the bullet train to Sendai. I had the Kilkee Triathlon in my legs, plus jet lag and travel tiredness, but Japan was wonderful and I finished in sixth place.

The NCF All-Ireland Triathlon was five weeks later and, true to his word, Pat Curley had lined up a top challenge. Mike Harris, the British triathlon champion, and a 2-hour-and-17-minute marathon runner, had the pedigree to win. Jim Bell from Florida had finished 32nd in the Hawaii Ironman, so he was going to be tough opposition too. Rick Conway, a top-class American, was quietly confident. Philip Gabel from Australia had the impressive credential of being their triathlon champion in a country where triathlon was already very popular, and he had just come from winning an elite event in Perth. And then there were the Northern athletes, who badly wanted to get their hands on the silverware and take it across the border. Suffice to say it was an anti-climax. I had trained too well. In Sligo that day I felt invincible. I had completed the full Half Ironman course in 4 hours, 4 minutes and 41 seconds – cycling a full 10 minutes faster than the finisher in second place, the British champion Mike Harris. I was in peak shape, and I couldn't wait to get back into training for five weeks' time when I would compete in the World Triathlon Championships in Nice.

The top athletes from all over the world were signed up for that event. It was the first time that the "big five" of the sport would face one another: Mark Allen, Dave Scott, Scott Tinley, Scott Molina and Mike Pigg. These five athletes dominated the sport of triathlon and Ironman. Then there were a dozen more American professional triathletes, headed by Ken Glah and Jeff Devlin of Team Foxcatcher. The French had their star in Yves Cordier, and the Dutch had European champion Rob Barel and their new star Axel Koenders. Also present were the British duo of Glen Cook and Bernie Shrosbree, and athletes from Australia, New Zealand, Japan and, of course, the top Germans Yogi Hofman, Jurgen Zack and Dirk Aschmoneit.

Nice had not been nice to me two years previously. This time I travelled there two weeks prior to the event in order to cycle the course a couple of times and ensure I got to know every twist and turn on the notoriously demanding and technical route. The two-mile swim in the ocean meant my weakest sport would lose me up to ten minutes on the top professionals. Triathlon was changing rapidly. It used to be that each athlete had a weak event, but now the top triathletes were training full time and any weaknesses were being shored up.

My running, off a strong bike ride, was my ace card, and I genuinely planned on running the twenty-mile race in under two hours. If I could run sub-six-minute miles for the whole distance, surely I would record the fastest run and get up into the top six.

On the Sunday before the event, I cycled back the coast to Cannes to watch cyclist Seán Kelly compete in the Grand Prix des Nations. At the time, this was the world time trial of professional bike racing. A time trial is where cyclists race against the clock. I leaned over a fence and beckoned at Monsieur Jean de Gribaldy, the *directeur sportif* of the KAS cycling team, and babbled out a few French words – and moments later Seán Kelly rolled over to say hello, just before he rode out on his warm-up lap. Laurent Fignon showed up on his special low-profile bike, all high tech looking. He was the man to beat. Seán Kelly was on his conventional road bike and still wore toe straps; he rode around the four laps grimacing in pain. Yet he won the race outright, to add another Super Prestige trophy to his status as the world's leading cyclist.

A couple of months later, Seán was to undergo a scientific physiological test. His measurements came up as lower than many of his professional cycling counterparts. Scientists puzzled over how he could ride so fast. Seán was never one to talk up and he listened to all their gibberish. In the end he just asked one question: "Does that fancy machine measure suffering?" Classic Seán Kelly! Whenever he did speak, he always made sense.

To Seán Kelly, suffering was just another subjective word. One person's description of suffering may pale in comparison to another true disciple of suffering. Seán Kelly earned a good fortune out of suffering, greater than most of his fellow talented professional cyclists.

The first Olympic champion I ever treated as a physical therapist was Anthony Nesty from Suriname, the first black athlete to win a gold medal in swimming. His distance was the 100-metre butterfly, just 2 lengths of the 50-metre pool. Anthony was on a swimming scholarship at the University of Florida where I was doing my sports injuries practicum. He opened my eyes to the true meaning of suffering. I sat down by the pool side for two hours and witnessed Anthony follow a 1-kilometre warm-up with 100 x 100 metres, coming in at 60–62 seconds for every 100 metres, and taking off again every 70 seconds, barely getting 8 to 10 seconds to recover between each 100 metres. That was 200 lengths of the 50-metre pool at very, very high intensity. To witness commitment like that was truly amazing.

I asked Anthony what was the purpose of such a body-and-mind wrenching regime, and he answered: "To go where I or nobody has ever gone before – that gives me the confidence and edge to believe I am unbeatable."

I also had the pleasure of working with the Algerian athlete Noureddine Morceli from 1993 to 1996. At the time, he was holder of the 1,500 metres and the mile world records, and he became Olympic champion of the 1,500 metres in 1996, in Atlanta. I sat trackside at the University of Florida to witness him run 8 x 400 metres, running each 400 metres at under 52 seconds. Most amazing was that, after each 400-metre run, he stood in place for 60 seconds, hands on his knees, grasping for oxygen to recover. Then off he would go again, like clockwork.

He suffered like I had never seen any runner suffer. Most athletes jog 200 metres between hard efforts. That has the physiological effect of distributing and dispensing accumulated lactic acid. In effect, you make it easier when you jog between fast efforts. Not Morceli. By standing on the spot, he was incurring acidosis and lactic acid at the highest level. His strategy was to make it so demanding that it was mind over matter, suffering at its most severe, and he mastered it better than any of his competitors.

Kelly Holmes would also double over in pain during intensive track training speed sessions. Paula Radcliffe pushed herself to a point of suffering so intensely that her heart rate would reach 211 beats per minute, and the world would wonder at how the English girl with the nodding head could run the marathon in 2 hours and 15 minutes – a staggering 5 minutes, 11 seconds per mile – for 26 miles back-to-back. This was the product of pure suffering. Maybe non-believers of true, clean human performance should witness such suffering. Then they may become believers.

A number of years ago, Seán Kelly invited me over to Belgium and we joined the greatest cyclist of all time Eddy Merckx in a 90-mile cycling event. Merckx was nicknamed "The Cannibal" in his prime, and now he was in his fifties. Off the bike, he looked a healthy size of a man, probably 15 kilogrammes above his heyday racing weight. On the bike, he sat in the middle of the group like a grand marshal watching every move. With twenty miles remaining, all hell broke lose. The race for the finish line was on. Each cyclist was fixed to the rivet and there was big Eddy Merckx dishing out the pain. Going at 28–30 miles per hour, he had suddenly come alive. He was in the territory that excited him. His domain was pain and suffering, and he could call upon it when it counted.

On the physio table I have dished out plenty of pain to my clients over the years, and I have put athletes through seriously tough prehabilitation and rehabilitation programmes, to both prevent injury and expedite healing. I am frequently asked who of all the athletes I've worked with can take the most pain. From 1996 to 2003 I had the pleasure of putting the great giant of Irish rugby Keith Wood through many torturous treatments. On each occasion, I had to muster up all my strength and resolve to treat the great man, as the harder the treatment the better he responded – and he always won. He'd often shatter me, in fact, and I'd have to rest up and ice my hands after squaring up to him. Indeed, nobody I've met could come even close to the level of pain Keith Wood could take. Now that he is eight years retired and a little softened up, I can get the better of him, but in his day he would have gone through a brick wall for Ireland. Paula Radcliffe is well known as one of the toughest of all the great runners. She can suffer on the physio table like no other woman, and take it all in her stride.

I had to put myself through some pain and suffering at the World Triathlon Championship in Nice that October of 1986. It started and finished along the Promenade des Anglais, and I was having a cracker of a race.

The two-mile sea swim had been a rough affair, but I had a respectable performance. The 77-mile cycle course was one of the most demanding and technical in the sport of triathlon. I had one of the leading bike times, and arrived at the bike-to-run transition in 33rd position. Running out across the timing mat, I started my own stopwatch to time each mile of the twenty-mile course, and I tried to run just a shade under six-minutes per mile. I went through the ten-mile marker at just under sixty minutes – right on target. Running past athletes who had overcooked themselves gave me tremendous encouragement. The sun had risen high in the sky and the temperature was 82°F.

It was 2.00 p.m. now, with six miles to go, when I started getting dizzy. I had neglected to drink fluid, and, with the ocean breeze wiping away the sweat, I did not realise how dehydrated I had become. The famous Negresco Hotel, with its pink dome, loomed in the distance. It was a landmark I knew well from training up and down the promenade. It was still a good three miles to the finish and I was running, but slowly. I crossed the line in fourteenth position, having run the twenty miles in two hours and eight minutes. It was a good run by anyone else's standard, but at least eight minutes down on what I planned, which meant the difference between finishing fourteenth and being placed in the top six. I was hard on myself. My expectations were high but, on reflection, I consoled myself that I had progressed from 24th place the previous year to 14th – a significant improvement. "Roll on the winter," I thought, "so I can get my swimming weakness sorted out."

Mark Allen won the race. His running time was two hours and three minutes, and he once again proved that, in Nice, in his prime, he was unbeatable.

10

Reaching the Top of My Game

I have worked with over 60 Olympic medal winners over the past 21 years. Some I would not waste away the time of day talking to – and yet for most I would down tools straight away and value every moment in their company.

On December 1, 1956, Ronnie Delany won the Olympic gold medal for the 1,500 metres, and five years later I was born. Growing up, I would never have imagined that a man who I had never witnessed competing in the flesh would have such an influence on me.

As I mentioned, I first met Ronnie Delany in the Sligo Park Hotel on June 17, 1984, just a few hours before winning my first All-Ireland Triathlon. Ronnie sat watching me scoffing my face with a breakfast fit to serve an army, and he quietly chuckled to himself. It was several years later when he first explained to me that he reckoned we had something in common – and it wasn't the gold medal.

At age 22, when Ronnie was a student at Villanova University in Ardmore, Pennsylvania, he was often invited out for Sunday lunch to the family home of a fellow student. Yet, for an hour beforehand, Ronnie would have a full meal, unknown to his hosts. He'd then play hungry and eat another full meal.

That similarity aside, I was fortunate to meet in Ronnie a kindred spirit, a man who has helped me over the years as both a mentor and role model. Men like Ronnie Delany are something of a dying breed. He has the elegance, the poise, the diplomacy, the polished voice to carry being a champion of his people, and, quite frankly, he is the perfect gentleman.

I got to compete in Japan on several occasions and, aside from enjoying the excellent hospitality and triathlon competition, I gleaned a very important lesson from the Japanese people – I witnessed firsthand the respect and value they have for their elders. Even the poor old man on the street is respected and, indeed, streetwise, with an interesting story to tell and a lesson to share. Ronnie Delany is the elder statesman of Irish sport – it's sometimes hard to believe that he is Ireland's most recent Olympic gold medal winner on the track, now 55 years ago. He is a wise old owl, with so much wisdom to offer the listening ear.

I later started meeting Ronnie on a more formal basis at his office in Fitzwilliam Square in 1986, and he not only helped me with some sponsorship contacts, but, more importantly, he gave me confidence to think on global terms rather than on a parochial level. It was clear to Ronnie that if I could finish fourteenth in the World Triathlon Championship, while training in Ireland and working full time, I should give triathlon a full-time shot. Ronnie was thinking big, and thinking way outside the small boxes of sponsorship available in Ireland.

During his years at Villanova University, Ronnie got to know the American billionaire John E. du Pont, an heir to the DuPont chemical fortune. Du Pont had funded a new basketball arena at Villanova University, which was opened in 1986 and aptly named the du Pont Pavilion. He also built the state-of-the-art Foxcatcher National Training Centre on the 800-acre Foxcatcher property in Newtown Square, Pennsylvania – which was the original du Pont family homestead. Within the facility was a 50-metre Olympic swimming pool for the exclusive use of the Foxcatcher Swim Team and Foxcatcher Triathlon Team.

Ronnie brokered a contract with John du Pont to include me on the Foxcatcher Triathlon Team of 1988. I would be fully supported by the team, including having residence on the site. Two of the top athletes who I knew from Hawaii and Nice, Kenny Glah and Jeff Devlin, were already Team Foxcatcher athletes. It was all very interesting and promising. A few loose ends had to be tied up, but I started looking forward to the 1987 Triathlon season with renewed vigour. I believed that, with a structured training programme, away from the duress of fitting training in around a full working day and standing on my feet serving customers, I could certainly go a lot further in this sport.

In the spring of 1987, I increased the training volume and took part in two short course triathlons – which I won easily – before going back to Japan for the Japanese International Triathlon. One of those short course triathlons was the Cork Triathlon, three weeks before the trip to Japan – and such was my focus that, on the morning of the Cork race, I cycled the 60 miles from Limerick to Cork, won the triathlon by 4 minutes, and cycled 30 miles back towards Limerick, before eventually taking a lift home the rest of the way.

The Japanese Triathlon was on June 28, 1987, three weeks before the Kilkee Triathlon and nine weeks before the All-Ireland Triathlon in Sligo. The event was staged in the city of Nihondaira, and I set a new record for the fastest 10-kilometre run in a triathlon yet recorded. After a sluggish but much improved 1,500-metre swim in 20 minutes flat, still 3 minutes behind the leaders, I cycled strongly to move up to ninth place after the 40-kilometre bike ride, then ran the race of my life to record 31 minutes and 4 seconds for the 10-kilometre run, and with that finished in third place overall, just half a minute outside winning the race outright.

I was reaching a new level and the future looked bright. The athlete one place behind me, Scott Molina, later went on to win the Hawaii Ironman, although shortly afterwards dramatically failed a drugs test. He also revealed a special piece of equipment in Japan that the world had not seen beforehand. Thankfully, Molina did not introduce me to performance-enhancing drugs, but he did spend time showing me his peculiar cow-horn handlebars on his bike. At the time I thought they looked hideous, but I was intrigued. They were total prototypes, made from plumber's piping and simply welded together, designed by Boone Lennon of Scott USA. Lennon worked as a designer of down-hill skiing equipment for Scott USA, but he also had a fascination with cycling and time trial events, and trying to pioneer equipment to cheat the wind.

Lennon made up a prototype of the handlebars and tried to get local cyclists to experiment using them, but most of these cyclists were too moulded in conventional ways and sneered at these cow horn contraptions. But not Scott Molina. Triathlon was getting very competitive and very fast, and, legal or not, Molina tried out the cow-horn aerodynamic handlebars – which later become known as tri-bars or time trial bars.

Molina gave me Boone Lennon's phone number in California and ten days later a delivery came to my door from DHL. My handlebars had arrived. My local bike mechanic John Loughran, at Siopa Rothar in Limerick, wasn't convinced, but he fitted them to my bicycle stem, having to cut up an old can of Coke to use as shimming, as the copper pipe was narrower than the circumference of the stem. But, with that, they were attached to my bike, and I was the first triathlete in Europe to sport these tri-bars.

Two years later in the Tour de France, French man Laurent Fignon had a 52-second lead on Greg LeMond going into the final day, which happened to be a time trial. LeMond was the blonde American, the outsider, and he had a secret ace up his sleeve that nobody saw until he rolled out on the time trial course. He cheated the wind with his clip-on time trial bars, clawed back the time deficit and actually won by eight seconds – the closest margin in Tour de France history.

LeMond, a world road-race champion in 1983 and 1989, and a three-time Tour de France winner, became an icon of the cycling world. He has shown to me how small the world is when connected by sport. LeMond and his wife Kathy have come to Limerick for the past four years. He rides the BDO charity fundraising cycle from Limerick to Doonbeg, stays and holidays at Doonbeg Golf Resort and walks the promenade in Kilkee, a stone's throw from Doonbeg. We have named the fitness studio beside my sports injury clinic at the University Arena at the University of Limerick "The Greg LeMond Fitness Suite", and he recently donated ten LeMond revolution cycle trainers to the centre – a champion in sport, a champion in life.

Cycling is rooted in rules and regulations. The world governing body of cycling, the Union Cycliste Internationale (UCI), has actively and consistently stymied the march of technology in recent years, hiding behind the argument of the Olympic ideology that it should be the man, and not the machine, that determines the outcome of the race. The UCI clamped down on bike design – famously banning mono-coque frames and the "Superman" position, following Graeme Obree's famous homemade bikes with which he claimed several world titles and set world records.

Despite limitations, aerodynamic technology marches on. It is a never-ending pursuit and improvements can always be made. The prototype aerodynamic bars that I unveiled in 1987 were not the most advanced, and yet, ever since then, thanks to the aerodynamic advantage of such aero handlebars, saving time, wattage and drag in the time trial became the raison d'être for many serious bicycle manufacturers.

I turned up in Kilkee in 1987 for the "Hell of the West" Triathlon and, for the first time in my triathlon career, I exited the water first. I then produced a course record on the bike ride and won the race by over ten minutes. I was on fire, as they say – although it was to be short-lived. One of life's great ironies is that, just when everything is going well, things can fall apart very suddenly.

Edward Smith, then editor of *Triathlon Ireland* magazine, wrote this article in the lead-up to the 1987 All-Ireland Triathlon in Sligo:

Will the sun shine and the seas roar at Rosses Point? Which of the competitors will be last off the dance floor at the Sligo Park Hotel? Will Superman Desi McHenry arrive on his microlite and do the biathlon before the triathlon? Will ITA president Maurice Mullins really grow a beard if Gerry Kelly passes him or visa-versa? Will Yeats again turn in his grave as the All-Ireland Triathlon "tour" streaks past his tombstone?

All these are of course burning issues. But of secondary importance I think to the ultimate question of the 1987 All-Ireland Traithlon. Can anyone stop the unstoppable and prevent the Limerick locomotive Gerard Hartmann from winning his fourth title in a row?

I am in a good position to make an assessment, having travelled to the far-flung places of Clare and the sleepy resort of Kilkee for the Munster Championships last month to make copious notes, and I have to tell you that things don't look good.

They call the Munster Championship the "Hell of the West" triathlon. It was well named, but such was the hospitality and the bonhomie that there was little time for note taking. But the message was clear at a Kilkee event that is a son of Sligo and perfect staging post on the way to the All-Ireland Championship. Hartmann, not only helped organise, instruct and start the race at Kilkee, but he found time to win without ever using fifth gear by a huge ten-minute margin.

I can reveal further information which will give you food for thought. The great man unveiled a new secret weapon – a handlebar extension to his Raleigh triathlon bike which is undoubtedly the first of its kind in use in Europe and perhaps further afield. If the top American pros gave us the upturned handle bar, this goes further [by] providing a place to rest your arms – the idea being to further cut down the wind resistance. Hartmann reckons it could save him 2 minutes in 25 miles over conventional racing handlebars. From the front it looks like a charging bull and after watching it in action in Kilkee I have no reason to doubt its effectiveness.

For those who seek to topple the King from his crown they must realise that [as] his superb third place in Japan (which saw Scott Molina placed 4th) proved, he never rests in terms of perfecting his performance. But simply he is getting better and there is no reason why the triathlete who has put Ireland on the global compass should not make a top placing in the World Championships in Nice come October.

Now, being from the North, I'll be accused of bias by suggesting that his main threat will come from that quarter, but first let me deal with the talent emerging from the Limerick Triathlon Club as glimpsed at Kilkee. They again look very strong to retain their title in Sligo with Victor Hurley and Frank Nash who finished third and fourth but those are not yet within shouting distance of their inspirational leader.

No, it is to the North we must look and the person of Ards triathlete Tom Heaney. He has been a revelation this season following a fine 14th at the European Sprint Championships in Marseilles earlier in the year. He has been unbeaten in local competition and is now a very talented triathlete. The one question mark is whether he has yet the stamina to sustain the sort of effort he'll require over the Half Ironman distance.

The other factor is the American and English challenge. […] Watch out […] for Rick Conway and Philip Gabel from America.

But no one prepares better for Sligo than Hartmann and the best view the rest of the field may have of him is a rear view.

11

Injury

Limerick City quickly embraced the triathlon – and in many ways Limerick, or "Sporting Limerick", as it is known, is the spiritual home of triathlon in Ireland. With over 300 members, Limerick Triathlon Club, since its inception in 1984, has provided champions on the competition and political front. An amendment to the Irish Triathlon Association constitution ensured that the role of president of the association would move each term from province to province. Con O'Callaghan handed over to Leinster and Maurice Mullins of Dublin. Towards the end of his term, Maurice contacted me. It was going to be Munster's stint to provide a president, and in fact Maurice looked to me to take on the role. If it was not assumed by a Munster delegate then it would revert to Ulster. I was uneasy about taking on a political role. As Ireland's leading competitor, I did not want to wear two hats, and I was also waiting for the season to end to go to the US to start my new venture with Team Foxcatcher.

Maurice Mullins was pressurising me more. When travelling down from Dublin with Limerick Triathlon Club member Tom O'Donnell, a Limerick solicitor and now Judge Tom O'Donnell, I put it to him whether he would consider taking the role. After much persuading, Tom agreed to take the baton, and with that became president of the Irish Triathlon Association.

At this stage, the International Triathlon Union had not been founded. There were growing tensions between the US triathlon organisation, the Triathlon Federation USA, and the European Triathlon Union and its chairman, Con O'Callaghan. Globally, the sport of triathlon was

almost growing too fast, and the politics at the international level operated on a knife edge. The Europeans were leading the way in getting
their organisation in order, but the Americans were not exactly too
impressed. They considered triathlon their sport, indeed their baby,
and there was no love lost between the two organisations. A sort of
tug-of-war ensued, distracting the sport from the real issues necessary
to move it forward. Tom O'Donnell was later elected president of the
European Triathlon Union, and Limerick Triathlon Club was the top
club in the country. In me the club had the best triathlete in the country,
and it also had a group of athletes who'd won All-Ireland Triathlon
team and relay titles.

As I said, when things are going too well, it is time to watch out. I was
6′ 2″ and weighed 11 stone, 4 pounds – I was at my fittest. I had honed
and chiselled myself into shape by training harder than anyone else in
Ireland. On a Sunday morning, three weeks before the 1987 All-Ireland
Triathlon, I was finishing up an 80-mile cycle. I was within four miles
of Limerick City on the main Dublin–Limerick road, at what's known
as the Richie Clifford Railway Gates, where the railway tracks cross the
main road at a perpendicular angle. It was wet; I had my head down
propelling my machine at a moderate 22 miles per hour on a routine
over distance spin. All of a sudden, I was skimming across the tracks
from left to right, and I fell down on my side. I was grazed and gashed,
and I was shaken and a little shocked. But, within minutes, I'd licked
my pride and saddled up again for the short ride home.

I realised almost straight away what had caused the crash: when
lorries and general traffic stop at the railways gates, they keep their
engines on and oil and petrol seep onto the road. I had hit a skating
rink. To this day, I still bless myself every time I cross those tracks, as
the man above was looking after me that day. It was a small miracle
that on the main, busy Limerick–Dublin road there was no traffic heading outwards.

Within days, I knew I was in trouble. With any attempt to run, I had
severe pain in my pelvis and hip. I could swim and I could cycle, but
even standing in the same spot, while working in the jewellery shop, I
was twisting to one side to avoid the pain.

One week before the All-Ireland Triathlon, I managed a three-mile
run, but I was hobbling. I didn't have a coach; I had nobody to explain

my plight to. I stayed positive. I assured myself that I could wing it on the day. I could swim and cycle at full capacity and build up a lead of ten minutes, and even with an 80 per cent effort on the run I would somehow manage to win.

In Sligo, before the start of the triathlon, I was interviewed by Brendan O'Reilly of RTÉ. I told him there wasn't any competitor in the race that worried me. That much was true – I was not worried about another competitor; I feared my own ability to run. The invincible athlete I had been just weeks earlier was replaced by a façade, an outward face of confidence. Inwardly, I was unsure if I could even run the half marathon on a course that I previously made light work of.

Tom Heaney from Newtownards, Co. Down was having a blinder. He stormed into the run with a four-minute lead on me, probably wondering why I was taking so long to catch him but suspecting I'd gobble him up on the run.

Mile after mile, Heaney was given a time check. He knew he was no great runner, but after ten miles, when the four-minute time difference was still the same, he must have said to himself, "Keep it going now, Tom. Another three miles and you are All-Ireland champion." Well, Tom deserved to win that day. He had been training hard since winning the first-ever triathlon held in Ireland in Craigavon in 1982.

Should I have started, knowing I was carrying an injury? That is the same question I face frequently in my professional career. Should Paula Radcliffe have started the 2008 Olympic marathon in Beijing, coming off a sixteen-week injury? (She finished 26th.) Should Moses Kiptanui, unbeaten in steeplechase races, have competed while suffering with brucellosis in the 1996 Olympic Games? (He finished second.) Should Kilkenny Manager Brian Cody have played Henry Shefflin and John Tennyson, both nursing cruciate knee injuries, in the drive for five-in-a-row All-Ireland Hurling Championships in 2010? (Kilkenny lost.) Champions take risks and what makes them great can also break them.

Crossing the finish line in second place in the 1987 All-Ireland Triathlon was unfamiliar territory for me, but I had no idea that I was going to be eighteen months out of the sport I so loved, looking for a cure for my injury. It was to be two years to the date before Tom Heaney and I would do battle again.

Ronnie Delany phoned me to say he had some update for me regarding Team Foxcatcher. He was going to be in Limerick the following evening, presenting awards as chairperson of the Irish sports governing body Cospóir at a sports awards function. I was invited to meet Ronnie for breakfast at the Ardú Ryan Hotel on the Ennis Road – a stone's throw away from my family home. I was down but not out, although I had no idea that my injury was a chronic one that would put all my plans on hold.

I listened to Ronnie intently. It all sounded fascinating. I would be living on an 800-acre farmstead with trails to run on, a 50-metre Olympic pool and a gym. Plus I would have a triathlon coach. This was the stuff I dreamed of. In tying up the conversation, Ronnie drew closer and spoke in hushed fashion: "There is something you need to know about John du Pont. I don't know if you will have any dealings with him on a day-to-day basis, but I should explain to you that it is widely known that he is somewhat eccentric."

Later that evening, in the excitement of telling my parents all about my breakfast meeting with Ronnie Delany, I mentioned that John du Pont was "something of a strange man". My mother saw red, and discreetly made some inquiries stateside to decide if I was making a good choice in joining Team Foxcatcher.

John du Pont was a brilliant man, but he was unwell in the mind. Aside from sponsoring and owning Team Foxcatcher Swim and Triathlon teams, he himself was an accomplished athlete in wrestling, swimming, track and modern pentathlon. He was an ornithologist and wrote two books on the subject of birds. In fact, he is credited with the discovery of two dozen species of birds. He founded and funded the Delaware Museum of Natural History, which houses within its cabinets 2,500,000 seashells, innumerable skins and skeletons, and the preserved carcasses of 75,000 birds. He was also an avid stamp collector and in a 1980 auction he paid $935,000 for one of the rarest stamps in the world, the British Guiana 1856 1c black-on-magenta.

I never did get to meet John du Pont. My good friend Frank O'Mara, a two-time world indoor 3,000-metre champion and my college mate from the University of Arkansas, suggested I speak to David Swain. David ran track when I was at Arkansas, and he actually competed for Team Foxcatcher, running in triathlon relay events.

David Swain explained that the funding from Team Foxcatcher was fantastic, but that he personally had to stand all night in du Pont's bedroom, video camcorder in hand, videoing the floor as Mr du Pont was sure Gremlins or little creatures were coming out of the ground while he was sleeping. I had heard enough. Triathlon was my life, but I was getting a creepy feeling. The truth was that John du Pont suffered from paranoid schizophrenia.

On January, 26 1996, du Pont shot dead wrestler and Olympic gold medallist Dave Schultz in the driveway of Schultz's home, which was on du Pont's 800-acre estate. Schultz's wife and du Pont's head of security both witnessed the crime. He was out of his mind. After shooting Schultz, du Pont barricaded himself in the steel-lined library of his three-storey mansion. SWAT teams descended as negotiators tried to persuade him to surrender.

He was known to have an arsenal of high powered weaponry. He held police at bay for two days, until they disabled his heating system from outside. In the cold January weather, they effectively froze him out. Du Pont was convicted of murder and pleaded "not guilty by reason of insanity". He was sentenced to up to 40 years in prison. In his book *Off the Mat: Building Winners in Life*, John du Pont wrote: "All my life I have tried to demonstrate – probably because I had to – that I could achieve and win on my own as though my last name weren't du Pont."

John du Pont was found dead in his prison cell at Laurel Highlands State Prison, PA on December 9, 2010. He was 72. In 1999, Schultz's widow had won a $35 million settlement in a civil suit against du Pont.

I was injured; I was no longer Irish Triathlon Champion. The Team Foxcatcher opportunity was put on hold – fortunately so, as it turned out. But all this had scuppered my plans to be a professional triathlete.

Injury, no matter what sort, is the bane of all sportspeople's lives. But sportspeople are resilient. They find ways to get over their injuries faster than mere mortals.

In 1988 and into 1989, I travelled up and down the country, visiting countless sports medics and orthopaedic specialists, from bone setters to faith healers, to try to rid myself of my hip injury. One local jokester suggested that what caused it might cure it: "Go out and fall off your bike again and it might correct itself," he suggested.

When an athlete is injured, they will travel to the far side of moon to get their injury looked at. They will also listen to every mad hatter on the street if desperate enough. Mentally, I was in pieces. Everyone had an opinion; everyone was the one to fix it. My confidence and self-esteem were kicked in the teeth. I looked in the mirror and didn't see an athlete anymore.

Eventually, a phone call to Pat Curley in Sligo put me in contact with Peter Coe, father of double Olympic 1,500-metre champion Sebastian Coe. He suggested I see a podiatrist in Henley-on-Thames to evaluate my leg alignment. Inserts for my shoes were customised for me and I was sure they would do the trick. Month after month passed, and I would walk the half mile to the canal bank where the surface was flat, and there I'd try to run. Within three minutes, pain would make me stop to a walk. No improvement! Despair set in and the tears of frustration would come. My head was getting more wrecked with each attempt.

A full year had passed. Triathlon was moving on without me. Tom Heaney returned to Sligo and won a second All-Ireland title at his ease. He had competed in the World Triathlon Championships in Nice the previous September. He finished 85th on the same course I'd finished 14th, and his time was over 40 minutes slower. He still had a long way to go, but at least he was running.

I was up and down to Dublin for several physiotherapy appointments before Christmas. I'd get the train up twice a week, take a bus into the city and arrive for my physio appointment. I'd get hooked up to an electrical stimulation device and be left in a cubicle for twenty minutes. Then I'd have six minutes of ultrasound on my hip at the site of the pain. There was no way I could see these fancy machines fixing my injury, but who could I speak to, who would put me in the right direction? Surely someone could help?

On one occasion, I arrived early to Dublin for a physiotherapy treatment. I walked over to the changing rooms at Trinity College, sat down and waited for almost an hour. I'd been told Noel Carroll came by a few times a week to do his lunchtime run. Noel was first and foremost an athlete. He worked as the public relations officer for Dublin Corporation, but he had been a scholarship athlete at Villanova University in the 1960s, won three European 800-metre indoor titles and competed in the 800 metres in the Olympics. He was one of the father figures of running in Ireland, responsible for helping to set up the Dublin City Marathon. For a man in his forties he was fit as a fiddle, still running 800 metres in 1 minute, 52 seconds, and winning European and world veteran titles. Somehow I felt the inkling that Noel would direct me.

Noel arrived sure enough, and he gave me the direction I needed. "Physiotherapists are good for soft tissue injury, muscles, tendon and ligaments," he said. "But, judging by what you are describing, I think you have a bone out in your lower back and pelvis. Teran Synge around the corner from College Green is your man. He's an osteopath, and he may help you."

Indeed, Teran Synge was the man with the golden hands for me. He found that my sacrum was completely out of line and my pelvis had shifted, all due to the crash on the slippery railway lines.

By January 1989, I was back running some easy five-mile runs. My swimming had kept me fit, and somewhat sane, through 1988. I had been invited to compete in the Annual Heineken Galway Bay Swim from Clare to Salthill in Galway, the longest competition sea swim in Ireland – a distance of nine miles. I finished second to David Morewood from England, who had swum the English Channel over and back without stopping.

My drive and hunger were coming back; I had reached the light at the end of the tunnel. I was putting the nightmare behind me. It was time to knuckle down again and think about winning back my national title.

12

Back on the Saddle –
The 1989 All-Ireland Triathlon

People often ask me how I manage to be so positive and driven. They wonder how it is I seem to be up all the time, so focused and so full of energy. Having positivity and drive may come more naturally to some people than others, but the quality of being positive and driven does not happen by chance. I have to keep working at it, respecting and nurturing it.

A racehorse may have a laid-back disposition, and be slow to get moving and slow to gallop, but when cajoled, when warmed up, he may be able to run faster and further than the rest. Another racehorse may be biting at the bit, frothing at the mouth to get going, but that does not guarantee he is any faster than the laid-back horse. Horses for courses, as they say, but the person with drive, who is positive, who loves what they are doing, will nearly always succeed.

Being positive and driven has to be worked at. Any battery that is constantly on the go has to be recharged. A physical therapist working with highly driven and high-achieving competitive sportspeople has a rewarding career. But it is also highly draining in terms of energy output.

I have to stay positive and upbeat in my job. It is physically challenging working with my hands, but mentally tiring as well. All healing professions demand that the healer is giving of themselves in body, mind and spirit. It does not happen by chance that I am in my clinic at 7.30 a.m., full of drive and positivity. I am doing what I love and using a God-given talent, but it doesn't happen without effort. My lifestyle conditions me to be charged up, positive and driven. It takes planning, discipline and even some sacrifice.

I have a duty of care and a responsibility in my chosen profession, so being full of energy is important. People put their trust in me and depend on me. I recharge my batteries in a planned and methodical fashion. I go to bed early, for a start, and I am fastidious about good nutrition, such as regularly juicing organic vegetables, high in phytonutrients, and drinking two litres of water each day. I avoid negativity – particularly people who are negative or have a moan-and-groan attitude. I don't allow negative media or negative situations to drain my bucket. Taking half an hour down time each day to reflect, to pray, to give thanks and appreciate my talents, and not take for granted that they will last forever, charges up the spiritual batteries and emotional self.

I know all too well the meaning of *anima sana in corpore sano* – a sound mind in a sound body. Physical fitness and mental health go hand in hand. As I am well aware, there is a fine line between being the fittest man in Ireland and being finished as an athlete. Drive and positivity comes from life experience, from knowing how to respect and use your talents when you have them. Most important of all, they come from being truly happy in your own skin.

My friend Moses Kiptanui from Kenya, who has broken numerous world records in middle distance events, once told me, "We come into this world with nothing; we will leave this world taking nothing. Live life to the full every day." An upbeat positive attitude always wins friends. You make a decision about whether you want to be the man who wakes up and exclaims, "Good morning, God!" or the man who wakes up and exclaims, with a moan, "Good God, morning!"

My focus for 1989 was simple and straightforward: to get back to full fitness by July 23 for the All-Ireland Triathlon Championship; to win the event and bring the trophy back to Limerick. I had won three All-Ireland Triathlons in a row, finished second in one, been too injured to shake a leg the previous year, and now I needed to put the record straight, not just in winning the title, but also in getting back on the international stage.

Tom Heaney had won two titles. He was gunning for the three-in-a-row. Sligo 1989 was going to be a head-on battle of two titans. I had to keep my head down and let Tom take all the hype. When you have been kicked in the teeth, when you suffer a career-threatening injury, when you are left on your own to find a way back, you toughen up fast and you get smart.

There was nothing I wanted to win more than that title. I put a photo of Tom Heaney on the back of my bedroom door and every morning when I got out of bed, I would glance once at the photo and it fired me up to get into peak shape for the head-to-head battle I'd dreamed of. I returned to competition and won two sprint triathlons in the Limerick Triathlon series of events held at St Enda's Sports Complex. The Kilkee Triathlon was set for June 24 – four weeks ahead of the All-Ireland in Sligo.

Kilkee always gave me a yardstick of my fitness, but it was never an event where I faced true competition. It was a little too far to travel for the Northern boys, especially when they had a series of good triathlon competitions in their own province. I put in a big training week leading into Kilkee; and, in fact, the day before the Kilkee Triathlon I trained twice. There was no point in easing down.

On the morning of the Kilkee race, athletes rolled into the Victoria Hotel to check in, and those who had not pre-entered could do so on the day of the event. Tom Heaney, the man I was gunning for, showed up at the check-in; but Kilkee was not where I wanted to meet him head to head. For two frustrating years, I had dreamed of getting back to Sligo and having a duel of a race, this time without a hip injury to determine who was champion. Now I had a dilemma: to pull out of Kilkee, a race that was neither televised nor covered by the national press, or to win the race quietly, without any excitement.

Indeed, I considered pulling out, but I needed a race. Heaney had thrown me off my game plan, for sure. He came out of the 1-mile swim with a 3-minute, 30-second lead, and into the bike-to-run transition 3 minutes up. I knew he'd run like hell to beat me. My weakness was swimming; his was running. The Kilkee running course is three miles out along the famous Dunlicky Coast Road, and three miles back. Tom was averaging six minutes per mile when I strode up to him at the three-mile mark. His game was up, but he was in for a bigger surprise. When I caught him, I shut the pace down and tried to make conversation with him, even suggesting we run in together and keep our racing until Sligo.

He was non-committal. In fact, I didn't even get a nod of his head response. To have kept going for just one mile at the pace I had run the first three miles meant I would have opened up a full minute on him, and could have then run on to win. But, no, my instinct was to amble along beside him. I had seen enough; my yardstick had got a reading. We ran down the promenade side-by-side and, with 100 metres to go, Heaney sprinted. I did not respond, and he crossed the finish line winner of the Kilkee Triathlon and, with that, favourite for the Sligo All-Ireland. This was just what I wanted to make the All-Ireland truly worth fighting for. Later that evening, I ran back out the Dunlicky Road, plotting my strategy for Sligo.

The 1989 All-Ireland Triathlon in Sligo was set for Sunday, July 23. It was irrelevant who else was competing, either from Ireland or abroad. It was penned in the press as the clash between the two titans. On paper, we were neck and neck, as in Kilkee only a couple of seconds had separated us. It was shaping up to be a worthwhile duel.

On the Friday morning before travelling to Sligo, I got up early and pedalled out for a steady two-hour cycle. Approaching home, I jammed my front wheel into a pot hole and heard a snap. My nerves were being tested. The steer tube of my lightweight Raleigh racing bike had cracked. I got off the bike, took off my cycling shoes and hobbled the two miles home, walking on the hard pavement in thin socks.

I drove into town to the bike shop. The steer tube had a three-inch crack; there was no way the bike could be used. Amazingly, in the heat of the moment, it did not faze me. I went home and took out my training bike and travelled on to Sligo. When I arrived in Sligo and went out for a cycle, I found the chain on the training bike was well worn and was slipping on the cogs of my racing wheel. I left the bike into Gary Rooney at his bike shop in Sligo Town to be serviced, and collected it the following afternoon.

By pure coincidence, Tom Heaney and his dad ventured in at one stage and saw my bike sitting inside the shop – they saw my name on the top tube. Tom Heaney enquired: "What's Hartmann's bike doing here?" And when Gary explained that my racing bike was broken and that I'd be using this training bike, which was three pounds heavier, Tom went over, lifted the bike and exclaimed, "Jesus, that's heavier than a gate; there's no way he's racing on that."

But race on it I had to; I had no other option. It wasn't the first time adversity had shown its face to me and it wasn't going to be the last.

Tom Heaney had a superb start to the day – he was out of the water with a full four minutes' lead. On a superlight triathlon bike, he powered his way around the cycle course. He was clearly a man on a mission. Adrenalin and fear of defeat do strange things to you: Tom had known that I pulled back three minutes on him in three miles in Kilkee and then shut down my engine. His Kilkee win was at a price. He had emptied his bucket, while I had not revealed what I had left in my tank. I paced myself to a calculated measure. I set my stall out to pull back 1 minute on Heaney over the 56-mile bike course, and then run 30 seconds per mile faster than him over the 13-mile run, which I calculated would see me win by over 3 minutes. That was a conservative and cautious estimate, but in a Half Ironman all logistics can go out the window in a matter of moments.

Heaney had blown a gasket. He overextended his physiological limit on the bike course, going way too fast in the first 30 miles. I pulled up at the bike park at Rosses Point to see Tom changing into his running shoes. A quick change, a tap on his backside, and I commented to myself, "Now Tom, let's run and see who's champion!" I had waited for this head to head. The last time we had met in Sligo I graciously praised his win, and I declined to tell anyone on the day about my injury. I strode across the beach and onto the country roads with a new lease of life.

Sligo had been won and lost in Kilkee. Mind games in sport have always fascinated me. Tom withdrew from the race at five miles, well back on the road. I danced my way to the finish line – breaking the 4 hours to win in 3 hours, 59 minutes and 38 seconds.

I never spoke to Tom Heaney after the race. Indeed, what's fascinating is that, in the duels we had in triathlons since 1984, I don't recall that we ever spoke to each other at any length. We were two boys from the same island, north and south, with nothing in common with each other except the sport of triathlon and striving to win. Sport can be strange: sometimes it binds us together; sometimes it separates us.

That day in Sligo put the nail in the coffin of Tom Heaney's triathlon career. Competitive sport can be cruel. There are no courtesies, no easy wins, unless handed on a plate because of another's tactic or agenda.

Triathlon at the top level is a tough sport, physically and mentally. You put in so many hard miles on the clock, punish your body day after day and extract the last ounce of energy out of yourself to win a race. There has to be a point when your body rebels; it just won't co-operate anymore. When an athlete gets a stuffing in a race on a day when expectations are high, when the going gets tough and the body throws a curve ball at you, it is almost impossible to bounce back and have the same unbridled enthusiam. A bit of you can die on a day like that, and all it takes is that one bad experience to knock the stuffing out of you and you say, "Never again. I'm done."

My experience in 1987 of crashing off the bike and being tormented with injury for eighteen months certainly had me analysing where I was going with triathlon, and also what I was doing with my life overall. Yes, I wanted to continue competing and I believed I could be one of the best triathletes in the world. My ultimate goal was to win a medal for Ireland in a European Championship, World Championship or Hawaii Ironman event.

But during that period I was asking myself a deeper rooted question: what was I doing with my "real" life? Sport can tie you up in knots, in a false cocoon. Free bikes, sponsored equipment, paid-for travel and hotels, press conferences, photo shoots, interviews, racing the race of triathlon – but what about the real race of life? What about life without triathlon? Where to? What to?

I dug into my inner heart and began to realise that triathlon was only a sport, only a phase; it was about boys and their toys, and the fancy glitter of being an athlete, being a champion. I was not ready to let go yet, but I was searching. The deeper truth that emerged from delving inwards was the realisation that working in the family jewellery business in Limerick was not what I wanted in life. This was a bigger issue, an issue that tormented me for some time. I understood that I was the only son, that my great-grandfather established the business over 120 years ago. How could I face my parents? How could I do this to them? I would look like a fool and make a laughing stock of myself and my family by walking away from a secure, established business. What could I do? How would I go about it?

It is always best to face the truth sooner rather than later. Discontent festers away in you. My mother always drilled it into us that, if we had a problem, not to bottle it up, not to run from it, but to bring it to her or my dad's attention immediately. No problem is ever too big a problem when there is support. My mother knew, as all mothers do, when a child is not content. She could read me like a book and had been praying that I would get direction. But I had to figure it out on my own and come up with a plan. Only I could decide; it was my life to make a success or a failure of and parents can only do so much for their children. They, too, have a life to live and enjoy.

The runner talks about that unique euphoric state of what's often known as the "runner's high", when the endorphins are released into the bloodstream and you feel invincible. You have radiance, a glow; maybe you have sore legs, but you also have an increased mental happiness. Sex does the same thing, and that's why it, too, can be addictive. The same goes for drugs.

I always find it fascinating, when going on a long training cycle in a group, how most have their two large jumbo bottles full of concentrated carbohydrate drinks, plus their pockets filled with energy bars and energy gels, and all types of goodies to fuel their journey. It's like they need all that junk to survive. It's their crutch, insurance that they will finish the ride. I am the opposite. Maybe I am a masochist.

A long cycle is more of a spiritual, almost out-of-body experience for me. All I need are two water bottles, one banana and a testing 100-mile course. Nowhere, with the exception of being out on the Hawaii lava fields competing in the Hawaii Ironman, can I learn so much about who I am, what I am and what I want in such a short period of time.

On such a cycle, the first 60 to 70 miles are a breeze, but with only half a mashed banana left in the back pocket you hold on to it and ration that 3 or 4 inches of carbohydrate like your life depends on it. And it does. That is your life line to make it back to base. The legs weaken; the mind questions. You start to wonder if you can stay upright on the bike. If you stop, it's over – you'll never get back up. You must keep going. Body and mind feel like two separate entities. You are only half alive, only hanging on by a thread. It's a temporary state of being – nothing that a good feed of pasta can't cure – but still a feeling close to a near-death experience.

When you are in such a place, you draw on your inner strength. It tests you physically to the limit, plus your ability to suffer and to endure. More importantly, it tests you mentally. Like a sick person, you have a choice: you can take your chances, fight the good fight or throw in the towel and give up. Like the ill person, it becomes very clear to you what you want to do with your life and who you want to spend time with for whatever time you have left. You realise that you have been living in the comfort zone, taking the easy option, chugging along. You have choices. The reality may be hard to swallow, but the choice becomes clear on a long bike ride, when reaching home can feel a little like arriving at the top of Everest. You have not just finished a 100-mile cycle; you have found direction, purpose and something meaningful. You have found your true self.

13

Life beyond Triathlon?

Six weeks after regaining my All-Ireland Triathlon title in Sligo, I was in San Antonio, Texas, competing in the most competitive triathlon in the US: the US Triathlon Championship – a 2-mile lake swim, 50-mile bike ride and a 10-mile run. It was dry and very hot – 103°F, in fact. I had arrived from Ireland just three days earlier. I knew I needed to return to international competition to try to claw back to where I was in 1987, before injury derailed my progress.

When you are a weak swimmer, swimming in a lake can make you even weaker. The water is dead heavy, unlike the salt-water buoyancy of the sea which gives you some lift. Without a wetsuit, I was sinking to the bottom. But I placed seventh overall in that triathlon, and there was some life coming back into my legs again.

A few weeks later, I was in Hawaii on my own: no RTÉ, no funding, just me on a shoestring budget. One part of my mind was concentrating on the athletic feat ahead, while the other was trying to picture what I wanted to do with my real life. I was to get plenty of time on October 14, 1989 to tackle my demons.

I exited the water in one hour, one minute – an eight-minute improvement on my 1985 Hawaii Ironman swim performance. I stormed into a 4 hours and 48 minutes bike split, some 42 minutes faster than in 1985. A 3-hour marathon would have given me a finishing time of 8 hours and 58 minutes to 9 hours – still allowing 6 to 8 minutes for transition time. But it wasn't to happen.

My cycle time had been one of the fastest of the day, but when I stood up from putting on my running shoes, a bulge the size of my thumb protruded out of my stomach. I had torn my gut and got a hernia. The pain came on sharp and sudden. I could not run a single step. The gun was put to my head for the first time in such a situation and I said to myself, "Don't deal with the negative; answer the question, are you an Ironman?" The chance of a top finish having dissipated, I walked out of the bike park and bent over, clutching the right side of my stomach. I had made up my mind to finish out the day in true Ironman spirit, and drag myself mile after mile towards the finish line, walking all the way. I crossed the finish line on Ali'i Drive in 244th place in 10 hours, 44 minutes. I had covered the marathon in 4 hours and 58 minutes, a near crawl to me.

The performance at the top level in triathlon was reaching staggering levels. Ironman 1989 is still considered the most competitively stacked Ironman ever. It was a dramatic race, with Dave Scott and Mark Allen running stride for stride, mile after mile, not once looking across at one another but just focused on the task in hand. For eight hours they had been going at it hammer and tongs, not separated once by more than a body length. As Allen and Scott moved closer and closer to the finish at Kona, the thought of a sprint finish had to be going through each of their heads. At 24 miles, Allen surged on a hill and opened up a gap. He held it right to the finish line, having to run the marathon in 2 hours, 40 minutes and 4 seconds, off a 51-minute swim and a 4-hour, 37-minute bike ride. It was a truly awesome performance.

But that day stands out in my mind, too, in that my almost-great day in the Hawaii Ironman race still turned out to be one of the most important days of my life. Competing in the swim and bike ride had been all about pumping adrenalin and focusing on performance. Once a top finish was scuppered, I wore the hat of just another middle-of-the-packer, trying to survive a long, long day in the sun. That same day, I was meant to be in Little Rock, Arkansas for the wedding of my best friend Frank O'Mara, but I'd reckoned the triathlon and the Hawaii Ironman were far more important.

Walking along the highway, I watched other souls straining their bodies and pushing themselves to their limit in the bid to beat time, rob a second here and a second there, to clock a respectable time for the Ironman distance. Many of them were simply trying to survive. For the first time, I was out of the competition mindset; my focus and drive had gone. So I could observe. I started asking questions that had already been troubling me: what was this all about? It was only a game, a us-against-the-clock game, to achieve a time that today was sensational but in time would only be average.

There is no doubt the Ironman experience had been exhilarating, but I was gradually realising I needed something more substantial, and more meaningful, in my life. Athletes, at the best of times, can be self-ish, and I could see that in myself. Life gets thrown out of balance as your every moment is consumed with yourself – your training, eating, sleeping – and with measuring everything by how fast you can swim, bike and run.

It took a few more triathlon experiences to get me into a more decisive mode.

Ogie Moran, the eight-time All-Ireland football winner with Kerry, was my physical education teacher when I was in secondary school at the Salesian College Pallaskenry, Co. Limerick, and he contacted me. He was employed by Shannon Development. They had sponsorship funding from Heineken and wanted me on board to compete in a triathlon in Tralee, which they planned to make into an international event. Ogie reckoned that, if it could work up west in Sligo, why couldn't they have an international triathlon down south in Kerry?

The Tralee Triathlon, set for June 3, 1990, attracted a large entry. I had been paid to compete, and £500 was the first prize. It was a sprint distance event. The swim was utter chaos; two canoes manned the water at Fenit, while swimmers tried to navigate around moored boats. I got out of the water with a minute lead, leaving Eamonn McConvey from the North and better swimmers behind.

I had a lead of five minutes when the police lead car failed to see the course marshal directing traffic left around the town to the bike-to-run transition at Tralee Sports and Fitness Centre. The Garda car went the wrong way up a one-way street and got jammed in by traffic coming the opposite way. I was practically on top of his back bumper, stopped in my tracks and waiting for him to get moving. I came up beside the car and banged on the Garda's window. The window was let down. I shouted, "For Christ's sake, where are you going?"

The Garda looked dumbfounded and replied, "I'm lost!" He was a blow-in on duty for the day and hadn't a clue. By the time we had re-routed, five athletes had got going on the run. I kept my cool, put it down as a bad day and stood at the finish line with Ogie Moran cheering in the winners.

The Kilkee Triathlon that year would serve as the National Championships International Distance Qualifier for the upcoming European Championship. The top Northern Ireland athletes travelled down for the race. Tom Heaney had distanced himself from the sport, but Noel Munnis came second and Kevin Morgan third, and I won it by cycling the 28-mile hilly course in 1 hour and 7 minutes, and then just cruising on the run.

The All-Ireland Triathlon in Sligo, four weeks later, was a race that showed up bad sportsmanship at its ultimate. The field at the top end was the weakest for many years. I came out of the swim in fifth place and flew through the transition area and onto my bike to get out on the road a close second. Within a few pedal strokes, I knew there was something wrong. I dismounted, centred the back wheel and got going again, but the wheel was rubbing against the brake blocks. I was cycling with the handbrake on. While the swim was on, someone had sabotaged my bike, nipping two spokes on my back wheel with cutters.

I have my ideas who orchestrated the mean trick, and a number of years later, while I was on a cycling trip, I met a former competitor from Belfast. He himself was in the water competing at the time, so had no evidence, but he relayed that it was common knowledge in his neck of the woods who had "got Hartmann".

Sport is not always straightforward; sometimes it can be dirty like that. I decided at the 1990 All-Ireland Triathlon to get back to Florida and put my head into the books.

I may never have ventured back to college were it not for Frank O'Mara, the two-time world indoor 3,000-metre champion, who first spotted my talent in 1988 and encouraged me to return to the US to study physical therapy. Frank is always direct and to the point, with a dry sense of humour. He once stated: "Hartmann, you are like a big elephant in a china crystal shop, totally unsuited to being tied up in a suit and tie standing behind a shop counter. You know more about the body, performance and sports injuries than all the physios I have ever attended."

It was clear to me now: there was no turning back, no second thoughts, no worries about explaining myself. I had seen the light. I knew what I wanted in life. The year 1990 would be when I would put my head down and give triathlon a side berth as I adopted a new focus, and new challenges. I was turning my back on the family business. And going back to being a student at 29 years of age, with no guarantee of qualifying or of knowing what prospects lay ahead, was daunting, to put it mildly.

Frank gave me the push that I needed. I had the wings. I was like a juvenile bird needing a push out of the nest.

14

A Life-Changing Day

It was a Saturday in February 1990 and I was in the O'Connell Centre in Gainesville, Florida – a large indoor basketball and track arena. I was doing a practicum in sports therapy at the University of Florida, and I was assigned to the medical room along with four other trainees. Our role was to provide various treatments to athletes, from pre-race limbering up and injury assessment, to post-race massages and general stretching at the two-day indoor collegiate meeting.

A tall, lean girl wearing a Villanova University track top edged over to me. She was shy, looked about seventeen years old but was probably about nineteen or twenty, and she had a teenager's giddy disposition when she spoke to me.

"I know you," she said. "You're Gerard Hartmann, the Irish triathlon guy. I loved watching you on television in the Ironman."

She was injured, and had been for almost two years since leaving Cobh with so much promise. Yet now she was just a journey runner with the team, trying to keep her interest in the sport. She explained how frustrating it was to be in the US with all her friends back home thinking she was having a great time and living it up as a star athlete. She'd had stress fracture after stress fracture in her lower legs, and was repeatedly sidelined from training and competition. She was not soliciting any professional care; she was just a lost soul longing for a chat with a fellow Irish person and was excited at seeing a face she recognised.

I told her that in Arkansas, where I went to college, my coach John McDonnell singled out the injury-prone athletes and never allowed them to train twice a day. He would drive them in his pick-up truck the five miles out to the golf course, where they would train on the soft grass perimeter. She said she would mention it to her coach, Marty Stern, but she was concerned as there was no grass facility at Villanova. I urged her to give it a try for a few months, that surely there was a golf course within a few miles of campus. She warmed to my concern. I recognised a good girl, stuck in a rut, and searching for a way to get back on track and use her talent.

I also told her to watch out for the golf balls, and shared the story of my college friend Keith Iovine and the accident that befell him on the Arkansas University Golf Course. It was a hot August day and we had stripped down to our shorts and discarded our running vests. Suddenly Keith was like the Lord on the cross, spread out flat on his back with his arms outstretched. It was a sight to behold. Coach John McDonnell ran down: "Hey, kid, you okay?"

A big boy on the university golf team named John Daly had teed off, the ball going over 100 miles per hour and hitting Keith on the ribs. We were in stitches laughing, and so, too, was my Cobh friend when I told her the story. Big John Daly went on to play in the Professional Golf Tour and later won the British Open, and the young girl from Cobh was Sonia O'Sullivan.

Little did I realise that, in just over a year, my triathlon career would be over and that young Sonia would go on to be a global star of athletics, and become like a sister and friend for life. A top-class person – and the greatest athlete Ireland has ever produced.

One of the advantages of being a student again was that, in some ways, it felt like being the full-time athlete. At the University of Florida, I had access to an indoor 50-metre pool at the O'Connell Centre, or an outdoor 50-metre pool nearby. I joined the masters swim group and, within a few short months, my swimming had improved to a much higher level. From always struggling in the swimming, I was now comfortable swimming 1,500 metres in under 20 minutes. With a wetsuit on and in the open sea water, I knew swimming was my new ace card. I met a professional triathlete named Cyle Sage, who in 1995 held the Ironman swim record at 44 minutes, 12 seconds. He had just finished a Master's in Exercise Science; he had the knowledge and was the inspiration I needed.

Time management as a student is key, and so my training became streamlined and focused. Each bike ride and run had a specific purpose. I started using a heart-rate monitor for the first time, and each training session was scientifically measured and recorded. I also had physiological tests done at the university, and recorded a VO2 max test level of 87.2. The VO2 max text is the standard physiological parameter for measuring the optimal oxygen uptake of the endurance athlete, and my result was the highest they had ever recorded.

My body composition was chiselled to 5.2 per cent body fat, when measured by a submersion water test. As a student of physical therapy, I now had a whole new approach to training. I was learning about the human body and sports physiology, and in many ways I was my own guinea pig. Four- and five-hour bike rides that were mainstream in the previous years were replaced by fast time trial training and interval training; the weekly 25-mile time trial every Wednesday afternoon on a measured out-and-back course on Highway 441 was the yardstick for improvement.

Cyle Sage designed a training workout, where he assembled 10 to 12 University of Florida Triathlon Club members and, after a 30-minute warm-up, he had them lead out one minute apart to replicate a time trial, with Cyle always going second last and with me having to start motoring exactly two minutes after him. He called the university triathletes "Gator Bait", named after the mascot for the University of Florida, the alligator. My mission was to catch up on everyone, himself included.

It was powerfully effective, as it got me to ride in the time trial specific position at maximum effort, recruiting the very same muscle fibres as in a race. When I recorded 53 minutes for the 25-mile distance by May of 1991, I had all the evidence I needed that sports scientific applied training works.

I was now eager to return to Ireland in June for the All-Ireland Short Course Triathlon, to be staged in Kilkee. Kevin Morgan had won the Sligo Triathlon the previous year and came in second in Kilkee, but my cycling was at a completely new level. I cycled the 28-mile distance close to 5 minutes faster than Morgan and ran the 10 kilometres at a canter to win the event at my ease.

The All-Ireland Triathlon in Sligo was on August 18 and, aside from wanting to put my new-found swimming form to use, I knew I had reached a peak in my cycling too. On the day of the race, I had my sister stand beside my bicycle to guard against any potential sabotage. I left my normal cycling and running shoes and attire beside my bike, but for extra caution I also put extra gear beside the bike of fellow triathlete Timmy McCarthy's. I was ahead of any unsporting types this time. My good friend Pat Curley, Timmy McCarthy and my family were the only ones who knew what had happened the previous year. I just told everyone else that my bike had mechanical problems. There was no value in giving the cheaters any satisfaction.

As Pat Curley used to say to me, "Gerard, my man, your ears should be burning. When they are talking about you, you must be doing something right. When they're sniping at you, you must be doing something very right. Never apologise for excellence. Excellence is perseverance in disguise."

Little did I think that a week later I'd be far from excellent, and it was going to take a lot of perseverance to get back to even feeling alive again. That All-Ireland Triathlon in Sligo, on August 18, 1991, over the Half Ironman distance, would prove to be the last competitive triathlon I would have the physical capability to compete in at an elite level.

As a race, it could not have been a more perfect swan song. I exited the water in front for the first time in a national championship. The next swimmer or two getting up out of the water behind me may have got a glimpse of my back, but within minutes I was powering around the course on the bike – almost as if I had a motor propelling me. I recorded a cycle time of 2 hours and 17 minutes for the 56-mile course, on heavy and undulating second- and third-category roads. The next fastest triathlete recorded a time of seven minutes slower. There was no contest for first place.

Cyclists dream for the day when their body and machine work in unison, when they can pedal with power and finesse and push the bigger gears while making it look easy. In fact, I suspect that may be why cyclists are tempted to take drugs: they strive for that moment when body and machine are in perfect harmony with one another, with the bike being an extension of the body, the two flowing as one – a powerful unit. On that day in Sligo, I experienced that unique harmony

– little did I realise that it would be the last day I'd have that feeling of peak fitness.

Happiness is a strange thing really. It amazes me how some people are always happy and self-fulfilled, while others are down in the dumps, all the time moaning and groaning about something. One man's idea of happiness may be kicking back on the couch slugging on a six-pack of beer. Another might find happiness sitting around the dining table with family and friends.

As children, we see everything in a good light; we are innocent and happiness is ours for life. When I travel into Kibera in Nairobi, Kenya – the largest slum in Africa with upwards of 1.5 million people living in abject poverty, with no hope and no future – it amazes me to see how happy the children are. As a child, I remember how happy I was day in, day out, with not a worry in the world, full of thoughts and dreams, and fulfilled by the simple things in life: standing by the lake shore and skimming stones across the top of the water; playing Batman and Robin; getting immersed in the world of Enid Blyton's storybooks. To hold on to just some of that happiness is the secret; keeping the spirit alight and alive.

I was always aware that triathlon was just a happy phase in my life, and that it would someday have to be replaced with something else; something purposeful and meaningful that would also bring joy and happiness.

In May of 1991 I qualified as a physical therapist. I went back to Ireland for six weeks, where I won the National Short Course Triathlon and the All-Ireland Half Ironman Triathlon. I was in the best shape of my life and I was glowing with happiness.

It is hard to imagine a road going through a marsh being the place to eke out happiness. The Paynes Prairie, a swampland just south of Gainesville covering miles and miles of wetland and vegetation, is not a place to venture out into. They say there are more alligators in that swamp than residents in nearby Gainesville.

Highway 441 runs right through the prairie. For two years it had become my regular playground. I trained so often and pushed myself to the limit on 441 that I'm sure I left a part of myself out on the asphalt. It was where I measured my day-to-day and week-to-week improvement; it was where I turned up to on a Wednesday afternoon with butterflies in my gut for the weekly 25-mile time trial that I treated as if my life counted on winning it.

It was August 28, 1991. I had warmed up well, doing 40 minutes of steady cycling. The temperature was in the nineties. The pressure was building up. I looked into the sky. Dark clouds were on the horizon – an ominous sign, in more ways than one. I knew I had to get this intensive interval training session completed before the skies opened up with thunder and lightning, because when that happens in North Florida on a hotter-than-hot summer's day, you'd better run for cover. It rains so heavily the cars have to pull over. The visibility is reduced to just seeing your nose. The bangs of thunder are so loud you have to have cotton wool in your ears, and that's when they say, "The Lord Almighty is angry." The lightning cracks its brightness against the sky and that's when they say, "Satan is on the prowl."

When I was seventeen, running back in Limerick, I trained with a friend of mine called Frank Madden. He was a quiet country lad, a few years older than me, but we both shared a passion for running. Frank always crossed the Paynes Prairie with me, not in person but in spirit. Years earlier, when he had just qualified as a curate in East London, he got caught out by a storm on an evening run. Frank stood in for shelter and the lightning struck the tree he was sheltering under. He was killed instantly. I always did my fastest cycling across the prairie, and I think it had something to do with the fear of thunder and lightning.

There had also been an incident with a local redneck the previous October. Cyle Sage and I were crossing the prairie when the side mirror of a passing pick-up truck hit my left shoulder. The driver of the pick-up truck had his window down and had slowed beside me, nearly knocking me off the bike. He put his head out the window and shouted, "Fuckin' faggots!"

In reaction, I raised my arm and gave him the American version of the two fingers, what is known as "the birdie". He slammed on his brakes, jumped out of his pick-up truck, and pulled a rifle out from the overhead cabin. Suddenly, he started shooting at us across a distance of about 50 or 60 metres.

Sage and I rolled onto the grass margin at the roadside and down into a water gully. After a minute or so, the redneck drove on. We picked ourselves and our bikes up, and we pedalled like two lunatics back to town. Our hearts were beating out of our chests for fear he would come and track us down. Never again was I going to give anyone the birdie.

On that day in 1991, I had eight times one mile done, each at an average of over thirty miles per hour, with just two to do. My legs were now crying out. The clouds were closing in fast. I could see the rain was bucketing down just ten miles south down the road, in Ocala. I needed to stay focused. I was travelling north, so I should have been okay to make it home before the heavens flooded me. I lifted myself out of the saddle, pedalling now at full power. The first ten pedal strokes at maximum output are what sets you up, like putting your foot down fully on the accelerator. I took a quick glance at the micro cycle computer: 32 miles per hour. I eased down onto the triathlon aero bars. There were 90 seconds to go – hold the speed above 30 miles per hour, concentrate, focus, hold it, keep it going; 30 seconds to go – I can do it.

I'm holding on for dear life. I won't let go. Then, in an instant, it happens: I hit something and hit it hard. My bike and I are sent flying up in the air. Traffic is buzzing along past me at 70 and 80 miles per hour. I don't know if I have any input or if the Creator above is looking after me, but my bike and I meet the asphalt in one big thud. Normally, when a cyclist crashes, the bike skids or skates along the road, and some of the impact is taken by the continued movement. For me, it was just one hard thud. I'm lying there in agony. I dare not move. I can't move. Cars start to pull up and people start surrounding me. One woman is clearly panicking, screaming like someone is dead. "Please, please go away," I cry. "I'll be okay…Just give me a few seconds and I'll be okay…Leave me alone."

"Medics are on the way," someone shouts.

"No, no, I'm okay. I'm okay. Just give me some time."

Next thing I know, I'm in the helicopter ambulance high in the sky, one eye half glancing down over the prairie, the other eye fixed on the blue-gowned medic preparing to inject me. There's an oxygen mask over my face, and between the painkillers and sedation all I can hear is my mind telling me, "Gerard, focus now, the last one-mile interval to do…."

I woke up in the North Florida Regional Medical Center, feeling less than half alive and completely unaware that I had left part of myself,

Gerard Hartmann, the champion triathlete, out there on the Paynes Prairie, on Highway 441 in Gainesville, Florida.

Triathlon and Ironman can give you so much, but can also potentially rob you of everything you've got. All sport, all recreational activities – from golf to tennis, from marathon running to rowing – has a definite health and fitness benefit. My involvement in sport not only changed my life for the better, but it made my life. I could never imagine what my life would be like without sport. So many people influenced my life along the way for the better: the Olympic athlete Valeri Borzov, who I never met, and Mary Peters, who I met many years later on November 16, 2000 in Buckingham Palace, where I was a guest the day she was honoured and titled Dame Mary Peters by the Queen. In 1992, exactly twenty years from the time he ignited a flame in me while I watched his performance in the 1972 Olympics on a black and white TV, I got to meet the great Finn Lasse Virén at the Barcelona Olympics. Words could not relay to him how much he had impacted on my life. These are just some of the people who motivated me, and there were many others who gave up their time and money to support my dream, most of all my parents, who must still wonder what they did to deserve such a dynamo in their lives.

Nobody in sport can make it on their own – support from people makes a difference. You cannot do the Hawaii Ironman alone. The Ironman is all about support from your family, your friends, your training buddies, your sponsor, your physio and your bike mechanic. On Ironman day, when you're out on the road praying you'll have a great day, you are not alone. There are 7,000 Ironman volunteers, working all day to make your dreams happen.

All that explains why I believe every child should be given the opportunity to participate in sports. They should have easy access to facilities, good physical education teachers and coaches, and competitive structures suitable for their age and ability. Sport brings out the best in people. It is one of life's great teachers. The downside to our technically advanced society is that, not alone are many of today's youth unfit, but many are very unhealthy. I know how close I was to being that overweight, unhealthy, troublesome boy who, because he was tall and goofy with two left feet, was shelved as not being fit for sports. Every child deserves a chance, not just a chance to play sport, but to make a team, to win a game and to find their true self; a chance to be happy and fulfilled. A healthy body in a healthy mind works across society, and can solve many of our so-called social health problems.

Every day, I see the benefits of recreation and sport. I also see the misery and destruction caused by unfulfilled dreams, and by alcohol and drugs. If it were not for sport I know I could easily have been influenced to take the wrong option. Young people can be vulnerable, through curiosity to experiment, through peer pressure, or in seeking to escape from pain and depression. I strongly believe sport and recreation is the alternative, and not only the best way forward, but the solution.

The benefits of sport are great all around. People go out for a recreational game of golf as a means of de-stressing or unwinding, of breaking the mundane routine of a nine-to-five. It is an outlet, and a healthy outlet. A father-of-two starts cycling two or three times each week, to lose the pot belly, to stave off the middle-age spread or to cheat the onset of old age. The novelty of something new and exciting, a challenge, a physical feat of endurance, the finisher's medal – these are all worthwhile because they are meaningful, and give status and kudos among family and friends.

But moderation in everything is key. The top-end high performer, the young twenty-something-year-old athlete with talent – of course they must certainly use their talent, explore it and maximise it. I know all about that, and how unique and special that feels. But to the professional career man or woman, with responsibilities to themselves and to their families, a word of caution. An obsession with anything can be dangerous, and sport can consume you. It can take over your life without you realising how badly bitten you have become. You might deny it, but, for those who are obsessed with training and participation, go to your shed and see the two or three bikes and the indoor trainer taking centre stage. Go to your wardrobe and see it crammed with running and cycling apparel. You have enough running and cycling shoes, goggles, kick boards and necessary pieces of sporting equipment to open a sports shop. Your food press is full of energy bars, gels and powders and the cupboard is full of vitamin supplements.

Like so many sports, triathlon and Ironman can become addictive. Perhaps sportswriters such as Paul Kimmage and David Walsh are right in their appraisal that all athletes are on drugs, in the sense that they are addicted to their pursuit. The more you get involved the more you want. Triathlon can consume you to the point that nothing else matters. You train, you eat, you train again, eat and sleep. Your work life, your career – that which puts bread on the table – becomes only a means to an end. It pays for the new bike and the travel and entry fees to the races. Your partner and children know you, but you don't know them. You are too self-absorbed. Your partner and children won't love you any more for winning a race or any less for not finishing a race, but they will struggle if your obsession robs them of their partner and parent.

I know all too well. I was that person. When I broke my hip in 1991 and went from being the best triathlete in Ireland to a near cripple, who cared? I was all alone. I had nobody but myself to pick up the pieces, to question what it was all about. Don't let triathlon take you over. It can swallow you up and later spit you out, leaving you with nothing. For triathlon to be a truly healthy and purposeful pursuit, it must fit into the parameters of a balanced lifestyle. That is the challenge for each individual – to organise the training, while keeping a balance in the other important areas of your life. Because in one split second, without warning, everything can be taken away from you.

15

Athletes, Stress and Health

Some people look at sporting events like the triathlon and the Ironman and wonder how stressful competing must be on the body. Is it necessarily healthy to be pushing your body so hard, particularly day after day over a long period of time? It is an interesting and, indeed, very valid question, and one I feel justifiably qualified to answer.

Sometimes I look through my old training diaries, which I have meticulously kept every year since I was fourteen years old, and I surprise even myself at the intense level of training I did over the years. I can't even believe that it was actually me, and I wonder how such heavy training was possible: 10 to 12 miles of swimming, 12 to 16 hours of cycling and 50 to 80 miles of running each and every week – and a lot of the running was on hard roads. It certainly was a long, hard slog, and I reckon even the best old Mercedes Benz would have burned out three engines with the volume of training I did.

All the professional athletes and Olympic champions I have worked with would have pushed their bodies to superhuman levels, and that does place tremendous stress on not just the cardiovascular system, the adrenal system, the hormonal system and the musculoskeletal system, but also the immune system.

People often forget the stress that training and competing can place on the brain. When I trained and pushed my body, day in and day out, not taking a rest day for months on end, I did it while working full time, as, indeed, did many of the top athletes at that time. But can that have been healthy and have many athletes I know paid the price?

I think of my friend Ann Kearney who unfortunately died from cancer at just age 51. Ann was Ireland's first true Ironwoman – a phenomenal woman for training two and three times each day, and who also took great care of her diet and overall well-being. My good friend Grete Waitz from Norway won nine New York City Marathons and five world cross country titles. In April 2011, she sadly succumbed to cancer. Great athletes like the American distance-running greats Steve Scott and Marty Liquori also pushed themselves to record-breaking levels, but were hit by cancer. Noel Carroll was the fittest over-50-year-old I ever met, and yet died a sudden death at age 57. My good friend Kim McDonald, a 2-hour and 18-minute marathon runner, who I shared many a long run with, died of a sudden heart attack at age 45. John Walker, the great New Zealand 1976 Olympic 1,500-metre champion, was diagnosed with Parkinson's disease in his early forties, as were three athletes I know. The list goes on.

I have thought about this subject in great detail, wondering if highly motivated athletes actually push their bodies to breaking point. I know I am no exception. What is certain is that the human body is not invincible. Everyone has a certain tolerance. People are born with a particular DNA blueprint, a genetic disposition and a congenital make-up, before whatever environmental conditioning comes into play. The human body can tolerate acute stress quite well, or stress that is short-lived. But it is not designed to tolerate chronic stress – the stress that lasts weeks, months and sometimes years.

But what is stressful to one person may not be stressful to another, and that is where stress and damage to health can depend on the individual in question. Stress is not a bad thing in moderation. It keeps us alive, keeps us motivated, and keeps the passion and fire burning. Some stress is good stress. Some people prefer to work under extra pressure, to be on the go all the time at a rate and pace that would completely distress other people. Their individual blueprint and make-up can handle it.

Distress is unhealthy stress. If the body is distressed chronically over a long period of time, it will eventually rebel and cry for help. The warning signs are usually apparent, but not everyone heeds them. Stress is a silent killer. The athlete whose immune system breaks down with chronic fatigue or with a musculoskeletal injury should heed the message from their body: "Enough is enough…you are disrespecting me. Back off – you are pushing me too far."

The body is not a machine. The athlete who trains hard day after day, without balancing this with rest and good nutrition, will soon have alarm bells ringing. These alarm bells will usually result in difficulty sleeping, when the athlete wakes up several times throughout the night, sometimes with teeth grinding or attacks of the hot sweats. Their digestive tract will be in a heap too, with symptoms such as constipation, diarrhoea, stomach pains and cramps. The stomach on a physical level will not function well and will lose the ability to absorb nutrients from food. On an emotional level, the stomach is fighting back, saying to the athlete: "I cannot stomach it anymore!"

There are other warning signs: muscles get painful and tense; the athlete keeps getting cold sores, and viral and bacterial infections; anxiety, frustration, anger and intolerance become frequent; the athlete loses focus, makes poor decisions, and can become irrational and negative and fixed into his or her way of thinking only.

When an individual is stressed, two hormones are released in the acute stage: noradrenalin and adrenalin. Noradrenalin is released when the athlete is angry and frustrated; adrenalin is released as a response to fear and anxiety. When the stress becomes chronic or lasting, the hormone glucocortisol is released. This hormone is only released in large amounts when the athlete is chronically stressed – but glucocortisol is also very damaging to the body and mind. The immune system breaks down, and a triad of health symptoms – physical, psychological and behavioural – will often result.

Over time, the chronically stressed athlete gets disillusioned as his or her performance suffers and more things go wrong. It can be a vicious cycle: the harder they push, the deeper the hole they dig and eventually everything falls apart.

In 1995 Sonia O'Sullivan was on the very top of her game, the best female distance runner in the world. That summer, she won the 5,000 metres at the World Championships in Gothenburg, Sweden. She was Ireland's Golden Girl – on route to what everyone assumed was an assured gold medal at the Olympic Games in Atlanta the following year.

She trained harder and more intensively for the 1996 Olympics than she had ever done before. She felt she had to. Part of her fear

was the emergence of the Chinese wonder girls, who had dominated the 1993 World Championships in Stuttgart, shattering world
distance-running records along the way. Stories emerged of their
mind-boggling training of up to 200 miles a week – or over a marathon a day – all the while apparently fuelled by strange foods such
as turtle soup, under the command of their truly eccentric coach
Ma Junren.

With that in mind, Sonia upped the ante again coming into 1996,
fearful that the Chinese were about to unleash ever greater ferocity on
the track. So she trained harder and harder, and dug an invisible hole
for herself. Inevitably that hole got deeper and deeper, until in the end
it was too late and there was no way out of it.

In the final few weeks before Atlanta, she won the 1,500 metres at the
Bislett Games in Oslo, beating Kelly Holmes and breaking four minutes
in the process. It was a superb run, but in the days leading up to the
Olympics her severe training finally caught up with her: she developed
an infection and a cold sore on her lip, and was hardly sleeping at all.
Then there was the infamous "gear row" before her 5,000-metre final
– where she was forced to change her vest and shorts in the tunnel just
before the race, due to a sponsors conflict – and with that everything
simply fell apart.

It took her over a year and a half to regain her vitality. The 1997
season hadn't gone much better, but after that she retreated to a new
training base in the mountains outside of Sydney, Australia – an area
known as Falls Creek. Up there at high altitude, away from ordinary
life and the hustle and bustle, there was no telephone, no distractions,
just a peaceful, holistic environment where she could eat, sleep and
train. It was there she also found added peace with the man who would
eventually become her husband, Nic Bideau.

In March 1998 she came back down to sea level with a newfound
spring in her step. At the World Cross Country Championships in
Marrakesh, Morocco, she won the short and long course titles on
successive days, the first athlete ever to do so. Later that summer, at
the European Championships in Budapest, she won a brilliant 5,000
and 10,000 metres double. In 1999 she gave birth to her first daughter,
Ciara, and the year after that, at the Sydney Olympics, she ran one of
the best races of her life to win a magnificent silver medal in the 5,000

metres, having been just nudged away from the gold by her old rival Gabriela Szabo of Romania.

Balance is king in everything in life. When I push myself hard, I do so to win, but in the past, in both my athletic and professional life, I sometimes pushed myself so hard that I crashed.

One such time was in 2008. It was an Olympic year and, with that, comes extra pressure and extra demands. Athletes pop up from every-where with their injuries, looking for a quick fix. Many of the top athletes I work with want the extra edge that involves training at altitude in remote places. In early 2008 I had two work trips to Kenya. Then, as the summer drew near, I had three nine-day trips to Font-Romeu in the French Pyrenees to work with Paula Radcliffe, then two weeks in St Moritz in Switzerland working with a group of Australian athletes. Upon return, I was faced with a three-day revenue audit. I went to Kenya for two weeks to fine-tune athletes there, and then came home for three days to rest up. Then I flew to Hong Kong and on to Macau with the British Olympic team for heat acclimatisation in advance of the Olympic Games in Beijing.

Following that, on the domestic front, I was moving into my new house with my wife, who was expecting our first child at the time. Weeks later, I was the physical therapist with the Netherlands team at the World Half Marathon Championships in Rio de Janeiro, Brazil.

When I returned to normality in November, my body was in distress. I could not sleep and I had a perpetual headache for weeks on end. Fearing it was something sinister, I had a CT scan of my head, which was clear. Only time and rest would cure me. The reality was that I had pushed myself too hard for too long. I had to stand back and take stock, and learn to find balance by saying no to some opportunities.

It is in my nature to push hard, to always shoot for the top. Winners win because of their super high drive, dedication and perseverance, and also because of their willpower and extra work ethic, but there is a price to pay. For some, that can be their health and, for others, their life.

I have not got all the answers. What I do know is that balance does not happen on its own. You have to work at it. The most important thing is being true to yourself; don't bite off more than you can chew.

If your work and family life is stressful then getting to the pool for a swim, going out for cycle or run should release some stress – but it should not become another "stressor". You can't burn the candle on both ends. If your work and family life is not stressful and challenging, and you have plenty of candle to burn, then give yourself a challenge. The good stress of a hard swim workout, bike ride or run can invigorate you, charge you up and fuel you with endorphins – and also reward you with having the functional capacity to improve and be able to enjoy your work and family life.

16

Beginning a New Career as a Physical Therapist

A couple of weeks before my bike accident in 1991, I was in Sligo on the day before the All-Ireland Triathlon. It was there I first heard the news that Seán Kelly's brother, Joe Kelly, had been killed. He had taken part in a 100-mile charity cycle and was cycling back towards his car when an oncoming vehicle hit him. Three days after Joe's funeral, Seán Kelly, always the professional, was back on his bicycle and taking part in a criterium event in Belgium. Seán had cycled every twist and turn on the roads of Europe at daredevil speeds, and in fact broke a collar-bone on a number of occasions. But it was his brother Joe who was in the wrong place at the wrong time. Maybe it's providence or destiny; perhaps life is simply all mapped out for each and every one of us.

After my accident, there was no way I ever saw myself getting up on the bike again. I had lost my nerve. The accident had rocked me to the core. It wasn't just because of the breaking of my hip, and the pain and slow process to get mobile again. I'd heard, too, that on St Stephen's Day 1992, outside Gainesville in Florida, a so-called redneck ploughed his pick-up truck through nine cyclists. Seven cyclists died, one was paralysed and one came out of it physically intact. They say when a redneck sees a possum on the road he "gets" five points if he kills it; if he runs a cyclist off the road he gets ten points.

Two days later, at The Oaks Mall in Gainesville, two young boys were out riding their new bicycles that they'd just received as Christmas presents when a city bus backed into them – they were killed instantly. Stories like that helped convince me I had my fill of riding bikes.

On March 18, 1992, I got a phone call from my mother. "Very bad news," she said. Joey Hannan, the life and soul of Limerick Triathlon Club, was dead. He had been out cycling when he was struck from behind by a drunk driver. Joey was only in his early thirties and was full of life and passion for sport. The Limerick Triathlon Club forever remembers Joey, and every May it stages the Joey Hannan Memorial Triathlon – which remains a great tribute to a great friend.

The stark reality of life without triathlon, the only life I had ever known, dawned on me the day I left the hospital in Florida. A friend came to collect me to drive me the four miles to her home. Jackie Ferber was a local physical therapist. She and her husband Corrie Landis had taken me into their care and I would be bed- and house-bound for many weeks in their home.

Getting down from the third floor of the hospital was a serious task in itself. Using crutches, I took it step by step, with my right leg trailing and all bandaged up. I slowly made my way through the long corridors to the hospital's entrance, where her car waited. It was a marathon of sorts just to make it to the car. I remember my shirt being fully drenched with perspiration from the effort and my arms were trembling. I was feeling and looking gaunt, frail even, and was almost afraid I would faint.

I must have looked completely helpless as I tried to mobilise myself into the back seat of the car, keeping the leg outstretched and trying to figure out what to do with the five-foot crutches under my arms. Reality set in straight away: I was an invalid.

I recall one long day, when Jackie and Corrie were both out at work, feeling particularly alone. I dug deep into my heart and faith. Fortunately, I had parents who were great role models and gave me the gift of faith, which I call on in my hours of need. As a young boy, I had often looked up to heaven in despair, especially when the rosary beads were taken out in the evening and study time or an all-important TV programme was disturbed for family prayer. We would all sink to our knees and pray the rosary. My mother's motto has always been, "The family that prays together stays together."

It was in this crisis, when darkness, fear and negativity tried to consume me, that I realised how grateful I was for having being reared in a secure Christian environment of love, faith and understanding. I had choices. This reality was not going to change. There was no turning back the clock. I looked into the mirror and saw a gaunt face, a body fading away. I had little stomach for life and certainly no appetite for eating. My friends were concerned. I weighed myself on the scales three weeks after the surgery and found I had dropped under eleven stone. My parents wanted to travel from Ireland to see me, but I was not ready to share the news. I was low and embarrassed.

Only three years earlier, I had turned my back on the business that my parents, my grandfather and his father before him had built up over 120 years. Managing Hartmann Jewellers and Opticians at 2 Patrick Street and 2 O'Connell Street in Limerick would have been a fine career for any sensible young man. Instead, I pursued a sport involving swimming, cycling and running, which at the time looked like being nothing more than a fad or craze. I had spent my savings and every last penny putting myself through college to become a physical therapist, and in one split second I ended up with nothing.

I do believe in miracles, but, more so, I believe in destiny, providence and in God's plan. What was to happen to me in the next year and continue to this day was certainly something I did not plan; indeed, it was probably outside of my own thinking or capability to do so. I am sure it was all mapped out for me.

After several weeks of feeling down and out, of not wanting or being able to fight the fight, I woke up one morning with a sense of finding a new light. I had prayed, I had cried and I had tormented myself – but I woke up that morning to brightness, to a life full of possibilities, and to a more positive, energised and driven self. What was to happen in the next year, and the following twenty or so years, was in many ways inexplicable, something that a PhD from Harvard wouldn't be able to explain or all the contacts in the world could not make happen.

The life energy that I had as a triathlete – the desire, passion, spirit, perseverance, focus and enthusiasm – was suddenly transferred over to my new life. If these were the inherent qualities that had helped me become one of the fittest athletes in the world, then they could also help me become one of the finest physical therapists in the world. The Tyrone football manager Mickey Harte stated, "My philosophies stay the same but I regularly change the window dressing." I can vouch for that.

The transition happened in the blink of an eyelid. It was seamless, almost like downing tools in one profession one day and picking up new tools the next day. Within one year, I was working at the Florida Sports Medicine and Orthopaedic Centre, one of the top Orthopaedic Centres in the US, now renamed ReQuest Physical Therapy. I soon became known there as the "Irish physical therapist" who was once a great athlete but who had a life-changing injury. People with other orthopaedic injuries, patients undergoing physical therapy and rehabilitation following spinal surgery, hip or knee replacements, naturally gravitated towards me.

I had my qualifications, but I also had had my own accident and many sports injuries along the way – so, even with very limited practical experience, I was in demand from the outset. To this day, I know that my accident happened for a reason. It was all part of a bigger plan. My life experiences – as the running scholarship athlete, the world-class triathlete and then the victim of an accident – gave me the insight, both physically and psychologically, to effectively treat my patients. I had been a competitive sportsperson. I had also been a post-operative patient who underwent physiotherapy and rehabilitation, and I had to learn how to walk again and cope with new challenges.

My work day in Florida Sports Medicine and Orthopaedic Centre always started at 7.00 a.m. and seldom finished before 8.00 p.m. I immersed myself in my new career with unbridled enthusiasm and a drive that was perhaps greater than what I had as an athlete. I had found my calling in life, and I knew it.

Sportspeople living and training in Florida booked in to see me; others travelled from far away. And some of these were not just any sportspeople – the world and Olympic medal winners Calvin Smith, Leroy Burrell, Carl Lewis, Linford Christie, Mark McCoy, Merlene Ottey, Liz McColgan, Grete Waitz, Moses Kiptanui and dozens more were among my early clients.

By June 1992, I was travelling as a physical therapist to the Barcelona Olympic Games. It was the first of five Olympic Games at which I have served to date. In 1996 I was the physical therapist to the Irish Olympic Team in Atlanta; in Sydney (2000), Athens (2004) and Beijing (2008), I was the physical therapist to the Great Britain and Northern Ireland Olympic team. I have had the opportunity and unique experience of working with over 1,000 Olympic athletes and over 60 Olympic medal winners, plus numerous world champions and record holders. It is a badge that I wear with pride and honour, but I respect that it is all part of God's plan and, like my triathlon career, I am aware that it is only on loan. To take something for granted is a sure way of throwing it away.

Every human being has been given gifts or God-given talents. It is a sin not to use them, and worse still to disrespect them. My name has become synonymous with the work I do with world-class sports stars, and helping to prolong the careers of top athletes like Keith Wood, Ronan O'Gara, Seán Óg Ó hAilpín, Kelly Holmes, Colin Jackson, Paula Radcliffe and Sonia O'Sullivan – and that always attracts attention and publicity. On a day-to-day basis, I am faced with the task of helping to resolve the injuries of sportspeople who are talented, who have dreams, who have big games to play and big races to run. It is a demanding career, because everyone who attends my clinic puts their trust and their hopes in my hands for me to resolve or find a solution. At times I do feel burdened; I feel the weight of their expectations on my shoulders. So I call on my faith. I am thankful every day to have been given a second chance, so I must help them.

I work with so many sportspeople whose profession is their sport. Take the Munster rugby players that I meet almost every day. Most of them are 28 or 29 years of age and know that their sporting shelf life will come to an end some day soon. When I talk with many such sportspeople, I see that they are already searching for the next step in their lives – a job with a bank or insurance company, perhaps, or opening their own business, and so on. I give advice whenever I can. I pray that, like me, they too will be blessed with something special, meaningful and purposeful to fill their years after sport.

Many sportspeople, when their careers are cut short suddenly through illness or injury, or being dropped from a team, have difficulty in the aftermath. Each individual deals with this in their own way. At its most basic level, it is the death of something that they loved and lived for, day after day, and often from the young age of eleven or twelve. They trained, pushed themselves, dreamed, all in the name of winning that club championship or intercounty championship, or that national, European, world or Olympic medal. When it ends, there is a void, a hollowness and a silence. Even if it is a planned retirement, there is still a void. When it is sudden, it is a big shock, and the stress that results can be detrimental to starting again at something else.

It was through my own accident and misfortune that I learned the nuts and bolts of what it really means and takes to put people back to full functional capacity following injury, especially orthopaedic surgery. My own experience and drive to fully rehabilitate after my operation formed my philosophies and protocols that I use to this day in my practice. What I learned post-surgery was that I was very much on my own to fend for myself. The surgeon who saved my leg did a fantastic job, but that was his job done.

After my accident, I was on crutches for sixteen weeks and hobbling with an obvious limp from muscle wastage and over-compensation. My left leg, the good leg, got stronger as it did all the work to protect and save the injured right leg. But I have witnessed over the years how little even the specialists know about what is necessary to recoup optimal functional capacity. People are told to do some swimming, some walking and to keep their weight intact. Too often, the direction is sparse in terms of post-operative rehabilitation advice. The reality is that, to succeed at post-op rehabilitation, the patient must work harder and more regularly than any guidelines advocate. I have seen so many people who have had a successful procedure at the hands of top surgeons, but whose functional outcome is limited, who are debilitated and in pain, and who are not able to enjoy a functional lifestyle because they were never guided or informed that it takes a lot of work to fully rehabilitate – a staggering amount of self-discipline and application.

Some people do not have the drive; it's easier for them to be the casualty, and live with dysfunction and impairment. In 1991, and for over a year after, I treated my rehabilitation like I was preparing for another Hawaii Ironman. I got up every morning at 5.00 a.m. and spent two hours doing a stretching and strengthening programme, plus other exercises that I designed myself towards gaining mobility around my hip and pelvis and the strengthening of the muscles of my torso and hip. Every night, I spent another hour stretching, always doing extra exercises to build up the weak leg.

As a physical therapist, my own career-ending injury gave me an education that all the theory in the world could not provide. I lived through it, doing my own intensive rehabilitation, and experienced the gains and results of becoming healthy enough again to complete the Hawaii Ironman and, indeed, run a full marathon. The experience shaped my philosophies and methods that I employ daily in my practice with sportspeople and other orthopaedic post-operative clients. In later years, I also developed what is known as "prehabilitation", or a programme designed to prevent injury and promote performance.

The philosophy that a flexible and stronger body is more functional than a stiff and weak body stands to reason, but the challenge is always to search for improved methods to gain optimal function.

17

The Power of Belief in Performance and Healing

I had grabbed the baton of my new-found life with both hands. My time as an athlete was a different life and I was a different person then. I turned my back on the sport of triathlon. A lot of my friends were in triathlon and I turned my back on them too. I did not have time for them anymore. I did not want to go near triathlon.

This was partly the result of giving my all to my new career. The desire to make it to the top in my new career had taken me over. The reality was that I needed something to put my heart and soul into, to absorb me, as a way of dealing with the past.

Triathlon had been good to me, but it had ended in tragedy and not on my terms. The ending came all too suddenly, without warning. Blocking out triathlon was a form self-protection, a defence mechanism. I blocked it out and replaced it with something more meaningful. I could not deal with my demons at the time, but, then, there is a time and a place for everything, as I was to find out. My demons would soon confront and deal with me.

In 2001, exactly ten years after my accident, I was back in Florida. I had been invited over to the US by Cyle Sage, my former triathlon coach and training partner, and now the head coach for track and field at St Leo University in Central Florida. The purpose of my visit was to be the keynote speaker to the entire student-athlete body, as they prepared for the 2002 season in various sports. My lecture was titled: "Why We Need Champions".

It was my first real public address to such a large audience, and my message was strong. I shared experiences from the "University of Life" to carry my message on why sport and recreation is so important, how it can save and heal, and how it can shape your life. My one-hour talk was followed by over forty minutes of questions and answers.

The following day, the President of the University and faculty members received me for lunch. They were delighted with my address and requested if there was anything they could do for me. I declined and afterwards I asked Coach Sage, "How many miles is it from here to Gainesville?" When he replied that it was about a two-hour car drive, I said, "Cyle, can you get two bikes? Let's drive up there and let's cycle across the Paynes Prairie."

We arrived outside Gainesville and parked the jeep. Cyle sensed the mounting enormity of the occasion for me, that I had a demon to exorcise, a past to overcome once and for all. "Gerard, I think you need to face this alone," he said. "I will drive behind you. Let it be just you and the Prairie."

It was a mere sixteen miles one way across Paynes Prairie. I saddled up, just wearing casual sports shorts and a tee-shirt, with running shoes and a helmet. I rolled out from Gainesville southbound towards Ocala, all on my own again on a bicycle and venturing into familiar yet unfamiliar territory. I was facing my demons. It had been ten years since I lost my nerve and now I was on the bike again, crossing the Prairie. I was fearful but I was also full of emotions. I had a fear that perhaps the redneck in the red pick-up truck would slow up beside me and push me off the road. Not today. This day was special. There were no armadillos crossing in front of my path this time. I passed the place where I had imagined a RIP sign at the roadside – the place where Gerard Hartmann, the triathlete, died on August 28, 1991.

I prayed ten Hail Marys, one for each of the ten years since my accident, in thanksgiving for being alive. Then I cried to myself for the next six miles, and banished all bad thoughts and fears. When I dismounted the bike, Cyle Sage and I drove south. He asked, "Gerard, how was that?"

I said, "Cyle, I confronted my demons face to face. They don't exist anymore. I now want to go back and relive the Ironman in Hawaii."

Cyle was taken aback. "Gerard, you've got to be in serious shape to do the Hawaii Ironman. You haven't trained for ten years; you can't run with your hip."

He was right in ways but, for my sanity, I needed to go back to Hawaii, do the Ironman and suffer for ten or eleven hours on those lava fields; I did not want to do some low-key triathlon. I had turned my back on triathlon, blanked out my friends, held myself to ransom in fear and deprived myself of being an athlete. I had treated myself like an invalid. The true test of my character and willpower would be to face the Hawaii Ironman head-on; to confront the most famous and toughest one-day endurance event in the world. I had been a prisoner for too long. I wanted to put myself to the test, to prove that, yes, anything is possible. To finish is to win; to win is to finish. So-called experts sometimes place limitations upon us, and thus we underachieve because of someone else's expectations, or the fact that they place the bar too low. From working with Olympic and world champions, it is my observation that most people, indeed many sportspeople, live in a comfort zone. Many people set the bar too low and never come near reaching their true potential in life.

Haile Gebrselassie, Usain Bolt, Sonia O'Sullivan, Kelly Holmes, Paula Radcliffe and the top champions of sport are champions because they set absolutely no limits. When Usain Bolt is asked before a 100-metre race to predict his time, his answer is, "I'm here to win. I'm here to run fast." For him or any great athlete to announce a time is setting a barrier.

Before 1954 it was thought impossible for a human to run a mile in under four minutes. When Roger Bannister broke the four-minute barrier, he shattered the myth. By the end of the twentieth century, the 1-mile record has been lowered to 3 minutes, 43 seconds, and I am sure that I will witness the 3-minute-40-second barrier being bettered in the not-too-distant future.

In 1993 I had the pleasure of working with and treating one of my boyhood heroes Eamonn Coghlan, who became the first man over 40 years of age to break the 4-minute barrier for the mile. At age 40 he actually failed to achieve this mark. He had injuries that did not allow his body to run with ease and efficiency. The pundits said if he could not do it at 40 he would be best hanging up his spikes, as there would be no way he could do it at 41. Over a ten-week period, Eamonn stayed with me in my home in Gainesville, Florida. He trained away, quietly and consistently, and every evening I treated Eamonn for two to three hours, fine tuning and manipulating every sinew and muscle in his body. In February of 1994, at 41 years of age, Eamonn ran a mile in 3 minutes and 58 seconds, becoming the first and only human being over the age of 40 to break 4 minutes for the mile run. To set limits is to sell yourself short.

Everyone has demons. Some of the finest athletes and businesspeople and celebrities I have worked with have hidden demons. People can be talented and gifted in their chosen field but have weaknesses such as alcohol, drugs, gambling or simply over-spending. Such demons may be the result of abuse or something bad that happened years earlier, and they can ruin a life. There is only one solution: confront your demons. Face them head-to-head. Stare them directly in the eye, and fight them. That can be through counselling, or through walking away from the stressful situation or the relationship that caused it.

A few years ago, one of the international top sport stars rang me up in a very disturbed state. I knew him well and had worked with him for years. He came to me and produced a registered letter, which he had just received. It informed him that he had failed a drug test. He pleaded with me to come up with some solution to get him out of the mess. He wanted me to formulate a medication for a musculoskeletal injury and state the banned substance was an active ingredient, and that the amount of this substance in the prescribed medication resulted in the positive drug test.

I explained to him the simple message I was taught by my parents all through my life: do not hide from your problems. Do not lock them up in a closet and wish them to go away. My parents urged my sisters and me to come to them straight away with our problems when something could be done, not when it was too late. My friend handed his troubles over to me. He admitted to me later that, if I had not been there for him, he would not have had anyone else to turn to. I travelled with the sports star to the residence of his manager, and together we shared the registered letter with him. The manager was not happy, but he understood human frailty. The sports star was hit with a six-month ban, and he underwent special rehabilitation to help deal with the banned substance he had consumed and his drug abuse. He then reintegrated back into his profession a clean man. He did not know what to do in his hour of need, but he found a solution to confront his demons. Everything can be dealt with, if dealt with sensibly. I always draw on Rudyard Kipling's verse:

> If you can dream – and not make dreams your master;
> If you can think – and not make thoughts your aim;
> If you can meet with Triumph and Disaster
> And treat those two imposters just the same;
> If you can bear to hear the truth you've spoken
> Twisted by knaves to make a trap for fools,
> Or watch the things you gave your life to broken,
> And stoop and build 'em up with worn out tools…

Be careful what you wish for. Certainly, 2003 was a year stacked with opportunity and commitments, and left me close to the brink of what my energy and time limits could handle. I spent seven weeks at high altitude in Albuquerque, New Mexico, seldom seeing daylight, as my days, from morning to night, were consumed with treating a group of great athletes. The most prolific was Paula Radcliffe, with whom I spent 4 to 5 hours each day working on her every muscle and sinew in preparation for an assault on her own world marathon record of 2 hours, 17 minutes and 42 seconds, which she had set in Chicago the previous October. A total of 25 to 30 hours lying on a treatment table each week, on top of running 140 to 150 miles, plus strength and conditioning sessions was the level of commitment that Paula applied to reach record-breaking heights.

People ask how I can treat just one athlete for up to five hours daily. Is it not counterproductive? And I would agree that, at times, I became overwhelmed by the intensity and magnitude of pummelling and stretching every sinew of Paula's body to make her tick like clockwork over the 26.2-mile distance. Whatever about it wearing out my hands, it certainly worked for Paula. She responded and benefited so much from this extensive hands-on treatment that she completed some of her training runs in eye-opening record-breaking times. The London Marathon on April 13, 2003 was when she would shock the world.

Several other top runners came to me in Albuquerque, ensuring that I spent several weeks stuck in a small apartment, treating from morning to bedtime, with no time for doing any physical training myself. Sonia O'Sullivan had been training in Melbourne, Australia and injured her Achilles tendon, and she flew to Albuquerque to receive intensive daily treatment. Elana Meyer, the 1992 Olympic 10,000-metre silver medallist from South Africa, had injured her hip and hamstring, and she flew across the world to see me. The US 1,500-metre champion Suzy Hamilton also flew down from Wisconsin and stayed three weeks, willing to wait her turn to get on the physio table. So, too, did US 5,000-metre record holder Bob Kennedy from Indiana, along with US steeplechase champion Pascal Dobert and Irish athletes Mark Carroll and Keith Kelly, who flew in from their training base in Florida.

Some nights I would go to bed and ask myself: how did I create this monster? Being in demand has its price, and there is no one more demanding than an elite athlete whose lifeline depends on staying healthy and injury-free. But it was all worthwhile. Paula Radcliffe ran like clockwork in the 2003 London Marathon, averaging 5 minutes and 11 seconds per mile, to achieve an amazing world record of 2 hours, 15 minutes and 25 seconds for the historic distance.

Back in Limerick after the London Marathon, feeling very unfit and with a patient list that had built up in my absence, I spent a full day sorting through stacks of correspondence and mail. Towards the end of a weary day, trawling through the mundane paperwork, an envelope with the Ironman logo on the top corner caught my attention. I opened it, slowly read it and just froze. Be careful what you wish for, indeed! Two years earlier, ecstatic after tackling my bottled-up fear and cycling across the Paynes Prairie outside Gainesville, Florida, I had told Cyle Sage that someday I would like to go back to Hawaii and participate in the Hawaii Ironman. The letter read:

Dear Michael Gerard Hartmann,

The Ironman Corporation has invited you as their guest to participate in the historic 25th Anniversary Hawaii Ironman which takes place on October 18, 2003 at Kailua-Kona, Hawaii.

Dumbfounded, I sat mesmerised for minutes, trying to figure out what I should do. I hadn't participated in a triathlon in over twelve years. I had not swum for almost as long, other than a splash in the sea on a sun holiday. When time allowed, I kept fit with a simple 30- or 40-minute run along the Shannon's river bank, yet in less than six months time I could be facing a full-blown Ironman...oh, my God!

It had actually been several weeks since the letter was sent and I had done virtually no exercise for nearly two months. A day later, I felt a cold coming on and a lingering cough had me sitting in the waiting room of a long-serving stalwart of the Limerick Triathlon Club, Dr Michael Griffin, at his practice in St John Square, Limerick. While waiting, I spotted the most gorgeous of gorgeous young women, an almost-six-foot beauty. During the consultation, I rattled Dr Griffin for a prescription to cure my cough, and then asked him about the long-legged blond girl who had grabbed my attention.

"That's Diane Bennis," he replied. "She's one of the GPs working here – a fantastic girl."

I had seen and heard enough. Once my cough was better, and after three days of pondering, I picked up the phone and dialled the number of the Griffin practice. I asked to speak to Dr Bennis, and asked her out on a date the following evening.

I had a patient list that would keep my hands and time full for months ahead, up to and including the 2004 Olympic Games. I had an invitation to participate in the 25th Anniversary Hawaii Ironman event. And, at age 43, I had met the first girl in my life who took my breath away, and who I would marry in 2006.

What more could I ask for but time – plenty more time.

This article, by Simon Lewis, first appeared in the *Irish Examiner Arena* magazine supplement on November 5, 2003:

For someone whose sporting career had been brought to a sudden and traumatic halt by a horrific accident twelve years previously, it took a huge amount of grit, determination and soul-searching for Gerard Hartmann to get back on a bike, not just once but twice in order to compete in the 25th Anniversary Hawaii Ironman Triathlon.

So when the world-renowned physical therapist crossed the finish line at Ali'i Drive at Kona on Hawaii's Big Island ten days ago, having completed the daunting 140.6-mile event in eleven hours seven minutes, the forty-three year old was not just finishing one of the toughest sporting tests of human endurance, he was closing a chapter of his life that had been left open since a very dark day in 1991.

He may now have a client list at his hometown Limerick practice, including such luminaries of the track as Kelly Holmes, Colin Jackson, Paula Radcliffe and Sonia O'Sullivan and over sixty other Olympic medallists, but, when disaster struck Hartmann on a training ride along a Florida highway twelve years ago, he was in his seventh year as Irish triathlon champion, having finished as high as fourteenth in the World Championships and sixth in the Europeans.

He had also competed in the famous Ironman event in Hawaii on two previous occasions, finishing twenty-fourth overall at the tender age of twenty-three on his first attempt. […]

Following his accident, however, Hartmann had thrown all his energy into his physiotherapy career, and blotted out all thoughts of the triathlon and its components. Until, that is, he received an invitation from the Hawaii Ironman Cooperation to compete in the 25th anniversary event. Hartmann phoned his friend Cyle Sage, the US National Triathlon Team coach and old training partner, to inform him that he had been invited back to participate in the 2003 Hawaii Ironman event.

"Cyle told me all about the 25th Anniversary Hawaii Ironman and how it was going to be a very historic day and how 25 athletes from the past were being invited back as guests of the event. It was always at the back of my mind and deep in my heart that one day I would go back to that island. I just didn't know when. It is a very spiritual event and for me there are deeper issues that I wanted to resolve. […]"

Having decided to compete and having told illustrious clients they would be seeing a lot less of him between June and November, Hartmann turned his attention inwards for some "me time". He had spent that period wisely; in fact, his preparations – including a mandatory Half Ironman Triathlon to ensure his fitness, his first event in twelve years which he completed in England – had gone great, he finished 3rd in the veterans' over forty, all came undone the week of the "big race" in Hawaii.

Of all the problems that could hinder him, it was one involving his nemesis, the bicycle. […]

Imagine what was going through Hartmann's mind when, a couple of days before the race, he was going downhill on a practice ride in Hawaii and the bike went into a major speed wobble.

"It was as if someone was shaking the bike violently," he said. "I took it to a bike shop; they took a look at it and couldn't see anything wrong with it. So, I took it to another bike shop and still they couldn't see what was wrong with it.

"So, that was fine, but coming up to Ironman race day you don't want to be changing your plans just before the event but my mind was playing games with me, my demons were messing with my head, and it just felt like my bike had deserted me and all my confidence in it had gone."

Standard practice for athletes in the build-up to an event such as this is to wind down preparations around forty-eight hours before start time and do very little other than rest-up.

Hartmann had wanted to follow that routine, but, despite the experts' clean bill of health for the bike, doubts about it kept nagging away. He knew there was something wrong with the bike and he didn't want to have it proved to him halfway through the 25th Hawaii Ironman as he descended a steep hill travelling at nearly 50mph with a tailwind.

"I wanted to ride it again just to make sure. So, I drove out about twenty miles into the middle of the lava fields where there is a very fast downhill. I decided to go down the hill at 45mph and get this thing out of my system. So, I went down the hill, but the bike went into a frenzy of a shake. I held on and pulled up because the bike, for some reason, just wasn't right."

Hartmann's instincts hadn't deserted him. Just minutes after he had pulled out of his high-speed test and at a far gentler pace, this time standing out of the saddle and climbing up the hill he had just descended, his cycle frame split in two.

"My bike was in two pieces. The bike shop mechanics had missed it, as it had been a hairline crack under the paintwork. It was probably caused by the impact of weight on the bike case during handling at airports, […] I had four flights to get to Kona....

"But, if I did not listen to my gut sense and own intuition and gone for that test ride, it would have given out during the bike race and, fuelled with adrenalin in competition, I would certainly have suffered a serious injury myself and probably brought some other cyclists down in the process."

The bad news was that, with a day to the big event, Hartmann didn't have a bike. Despondency had set in and he had thrown in the towel in participating in the event, until he visited the Expo Trade Fair at the Ironman venue. He went to tell his friend Cyle Sage, who was working on one of the Stands. […]

Opposite him was the Cannondale Stand, the official bike sponsors of the Ironman. Cyle Sage chatted up the reps, told them of his Irish friend's plight, coming all the way from Ireland as a guest of the event. Not only did they offer him a helping hand, they loaned him their showpiece demo bike, the prototype of the Cannondale 2004 Ironman Slice, which was to be launched the following January.

The only problem was the frame was the wrong size, not by much, but enough for Hartmann to go away and sit down over a coffee and discuss his options with his wife Diane.

At this level of competition, bikes are set up very specifically for the individual riding them and the bike the athlete has used for training for months beforehand fits like a glove. Every muscle and joint in the body is dialled into working in harmony together, bike and body in unison. The bike becomes an extension of the athlete, an amalgam of cycle and sinew, fused together by mile after mile of training on the road. You just cannot hop off one and climb onto another and expect the transition to be seamless.

Hartmann's borrowed whiz-bang Cannondale of the future had a 60cm frame and that could have serious consequences for a set of muscles so finely attuned to his normal spec bike – a 58cm frame with a different geometry. Riding that would be like a runner with size 8 feet racing in size 10s. So, on the evening before the race, he was left with a stark choice: withdraw from the race and walk away from months of preparation for an extraordinary event or go to the start-line, ride a strange bike and risk the strong possibility of his muscles seizing up half-way through.

He went back out on the lava fields on the eve of the event, test riding his newly acquired Cannondale, hurdling along Queen Kaahumanu Highway when he should have been resting up.

Hartmann would go to the start-line the following day.

"This wasn't about the race," he said, "this was about myself and the course. I think this was about facing my demons head to head and closing a chapter for me…" […]

Inevitably, the 112-mile bike section of the race caused the most discomfort.

"The accident of the bike cracking was unfortunate, but having to get on a totally different bike was both a mental and physical challenge. Over a 25 mile bike ride, I'd 'wing it' but straight on a new oversized bike for a full 112 miles – that poses a big ask. It wasn't until after thirty miles into the ride that I started to feel sore. I had to stop three times and each time pull over to the side and lie down on the blistering hot tarmac and stretch myself out. At one stop a motor bike with a Course Marshall pulled up and asked, 'Do you need medical help?' I snappily replied, 'No, Sir' and I jumped back on the bike and rode on. So I had to call on a lot of past experience to get through that.

"Having worked with great athletes, someone like Paula Radcliffe, for example, [I see that] she draws on a huge reservoir of psychological and emotional strength. All I kept saying to myself during the event was, 'Okay, get off and stretch for five minutes. The day will end. It doesn't matter how long it takes to do this event. Forget that you were a competitive athlete. I'm a Joe Smuck, just trying to finish the Hawaii Ironman.

"I kept repeating to myself, 'I'm here to finish this sucker.' That is what I came for. I didn't come to do a nine or ten hour race time; I didn't tune in to what anyone else was doing. It was just myself and the event, and on that day I drew on more mental strength than on physical fitness."

Hartmann came back from Kailua-Kona not just with closure, having completed the Ironman against all the odds and closing a traumatic chapter in his life. He also returned with fresh challenges.

With gold medallists Mark McKoy (Canada) (left), 110-metre hurdles champion, 1992, and Linford Christie (UK), 100-metre champion, 1992.

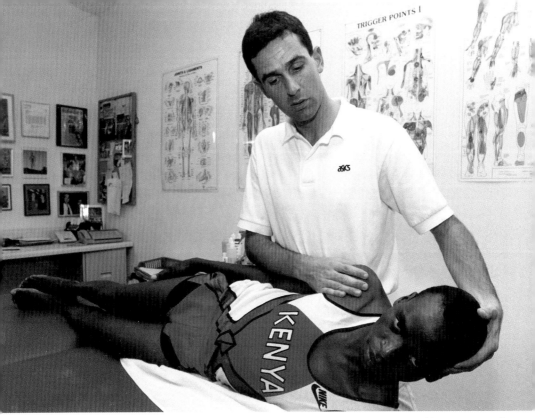

Treating William Sigei in Gainesville, Florida, 1995. William was the 10,000 metres world record holder and two-time world cross country champion.

With Moses Kiptanui (Kenya) in the Olympic Stadium at Atlanta Olympic Games, 1996. At that time, Moses was the multiple world record holder in the 3,000 metres, 3,000-metre steeplechase and 5,000 metres.

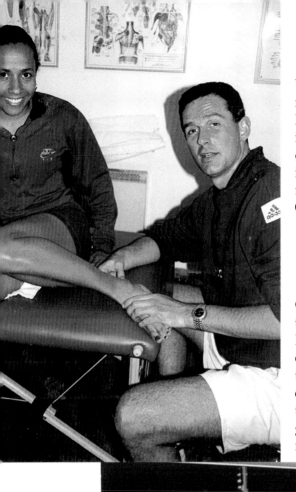

With Kelly Holmes (UK) in my clinic in Limerick, 2000. Kelly overcame multiple injury problems to become a double Olympic champion in the 800 metres and 1,500 metres at the 2004 Athens Olympic Games.

Crossing the finish line of the 25th Anniversary Hawaii Ironman in 2003 was a special occasion for me. I had been told I'd never run again by the experts and yet I completed the toughest Ironman on the globe, running a full 26.2-mile marathon in the process.

Ironman Triathlon World Championship
October 18, 2003

With my father Patrick in 2003. Patrick was an active sportsman throughout his life.

With Paula Radcliffe in 2003, minutes after she set a new marathon world record of 2 hours, 15 minutes and 25 seconds in the London Marathon. I have worked with Paula for fourteen years and shared many highs and some lows with her.

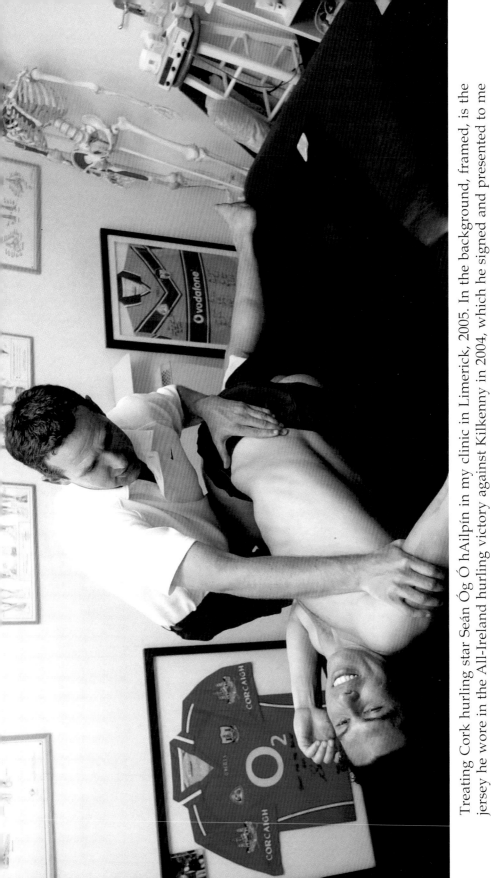

Treating Cork hurling star Seán Óg Ó hAilpín in my clinic in Limerick, 2005. In the background, framed, is the jersey he wore in the All-Ireland hurling victory against Kilkenny in 2004, which he signed and presented to me with the message "Thanks for the Belief".

With Kelly Holmes in Limerick, 2004. Kelly brought her two Olympic gold medals over to Limerick to share them with fans who had supported and encouraged her through injury stages, when it had looked unlikely that she would ever grace the podium.

With Ger Keane, my colleague at the Hartmann International Sports Injury Clinic and Ronan O'Gara in May 2005. Weeks earlier, Ronan came knocking at my door in dire straits. He had injured his right knee and he presented me with the task of mending him in record time for the Lions Tour weeks later.

With my wife Diane and my family on our wedding day, October 2, 2006:
my sister Thecla, my mother Thecla, me, Diane, my father Patrick, and my
sisters Leonie and Helga at Adare Manor Co. Limerick.
(*Courtesy of www.michaelmartinphotography.ie*)

Oct 2, 2006: close friends at Adare Manor for our wedding day: Frank O'Mara,
Marcus O'Sullivan, Kelly Holmes, Eamonn Coghlan, me, Sonia O'Sullivan
and Nic Bideau. (*Courtesy of www.michaelmartinphotography.ie*)

With Kerry footballers on the Tuesday before the All-Ireland football final in September 2006 against Mayo, which Kerry won. The Kerry greats visited me for a final tune-up on the physio table: Seamus Moynihan, Eoin Brosnan, me and Colm Cooper.

Cycling in Belgium with Eddy Merckx in 2007. Eddy is a five-time Tour de France winner and arguably the world's greatest ever cyclist.

"All together now" – putting a group of international athletes through their warm-up programme, Iten, Kenya, 2009. The Kenyans train in groups with the motto "Train hard, win easy."

With my wife Diane, a GP in Limerick.

With my son Patrick, who has brought great joy and fun into my life.

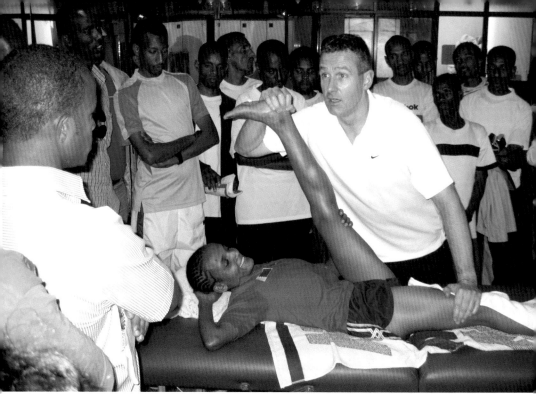

Teaching a group of physiotherapists in Addis Ababa, Ethiopia in 2009. The week-long seminar was exhausting, but the satisfaction of helping others made it all worthwhile.

In my clinic in Iten, Kenya in 2010, with two of today's stars: Mo Farah (UK) (left) – world champion 5,000 metres 2011 – and Joseph Ebuya (Kenya), world cross country champion 2010.

With Kilkenny star hurler Henry Shefflin in 2010. Henry's drive to win and excel is truly remarkable. In my view, he ranks with the best of the world and Olympic champions I have treated. An inspiration!

With Moses Kipsiro (Uganda) in my clinic in Iten, Kenya in 2011. Moses won the Commonwealth 5,000- and 10,000-metre Championships in 2010, and weeks later became the first athlete since Ben Jipcho (Kenya) in 1973 to win the 5,000- and 10,000-metre double at the All-African Championships.

Treating Vivian Cheruiyot (Kenya) in my clinic in Iten, Kenya, in 2011. Vivian is the world 5,000-metre champion (2009 and 2011), world 10,000-metre champion (2011) and world cross country champion (2011).

With University of Limerick President Professor Don Barry and Ronnie Delany at opening of the "Hartmann Collection" at the university in 2007. (© Press 22: www.press22.ie)

With Mickey Harte, the great Tyrone football manager, and Ger Keane in April 2011. Mickey and the Tyrone football team had come for a two-day training seminar in my clinic at the University of Limerick.

Cycling the Marmotte, July 3, 2009. After almost 8 hrs of cycling, I race the 9 miles and 21 hairpin bends to the top of Alpe d'Huez to win a gold medal for the 45- to 50-year-old category.

18

Overcoming Injury –
Kelly Holmes and Seán Óg Ó hAilpín

Day in day out, I get asked about the Olympics. In my teenage and young athletic years, I dreamed about competing in the Olympic Games, and wearing the green singlet with the shamrock emblazoned on it. I thought that my legs and athletic talent, along with training like a zealot, would surely secure my entry into the world's greatest extravaganza.

In 1991, when I won a seventh National Triathlon title and was considered a world-class triathlete, I was sure I would get to compete in the first-ever Olympic triathlon event. The Olympic family observed how triathlon had become a truly global sport and it looked like the inaugural Olympic triathlon would be staged at the Centennial Games in Atlanta in 1996.

Indeed, when I broke my hip in 1991 and retired from competitive sport, I fast-forwarded my participation in the Olympic Games: in 1992 I was the physical therapist to a dozen Olympic medallists in what was to be the first of five Olympic Games I have served at to date.

As it turned out, the first Olympic triathlon was staged in Sydney at the 2000 Olympic Games, and I observed the race with delight, seeing that the sport I had been a pioneer of had come of age and was part of the Olympic movement – yet, I felt a tinge of disappointment that I was not participating on this historic day. My athletic talent gave me so much, but it was to be my role as physical therapist that would allow me to participate as a member of national Olympic teams. Yes, it would have been a wonderful experience to have taken part in the Olympic triathlon, but I get so much joy and satisfaction working with and assisting athletes to compete at their best in the most unique sixteen days of sporting glory that only comes around every four years. As long as my talent allows, I want to contribute and be part of the Olympic Games, because this is something I will always cherish.

Throughout my 21 years working as a physical therapist, I have often become a source of salvation for many sportspeople whose career has been brought to a halt by acute or chronic injury. For some, I am actually the last resort, and when they come knocking on my clinic door after having tried everything and everyone else, they pin their last hopes on me. Sometimes they are looking for a miracle.

One of my colleagues and friends is Alan Kelly, the Tallaght-based physical therapist, and better known in the business as "the Great AK". He has treated many of Ireland's top GAA players, and when a sportsperson attends Alan with a serious injury, he usually sits them down and says, "I'm going to give you my very best shot at fixing your injury. If I can't fix it I'm sending you down to Limerick to see the best there is. And if he can't fix it, I'm sending you to Lourdes."

When an athlete is injured, the physical implications are obvious – but fellow athletes, friends, family members and colleagues will be also concerned, wondering how painful the injury is, how the athlete is recovering and how soon they will be back to their sport. So it is always more than the injured part of the body that is hurting; the person inside is also in pain – and that's an aspect that an athlete is rarely asked about. With injury comes grief, which could consist of anger, depression, fear or frustration. There is a sense of loss. The injured athlete is backed into a corner, and their very identity is rocked and threatened to the core.

Sport not only forms part of an athlete's life – it is their life. This is not just in terms of time invested in training and competing, but often their friends and support structures are based on the athlete being fit and physically capable. Sport and training forms a part of the athlete's everyday life, and without it the routine is broken. Suddenly their main source of stress relief or escape from the world disappears, and the athlete misses the positive daily experiences gained through the act of physical training or competing. That element of the sporting injury is often overlooked.

The athlete who is injured is like a bird trying to fly with a broken wing. The emotional rollercoaster that some injured athletes experience includes feelings of denial, anger, bargaining and depression. The final stage of the emotional process is acceptance: only when the athlete truly accepts that they are fully grounded and in trouble can they hand over the responsibility of the injury to the physical therapist or other specialist medic.

The great Irish middle-distance runner Noel Carroll completed an ironic circle by turning to me for treatment after he had once guided me with my various injury problems. He summed up my contribution to injured sportspeople in an interview with the *Irish Runner* magazine in May 1993:

> Gerard possesses a rare combination of qualities. He inspires trust. He has an almost missionary zeal for what he is doing. He also contributes an additional philosophical basis to the various disciplines he brings together. When the average medic sees figures, Gerard Hartmann sees an athlete. He has been through it himself. You don't just see him once; he manages the injured athlete through a condition looking at everything, your weaknesses, strengths how you sit and stand. He is providing a service that very few others offer.[3]

A number of years ago, an old man stopped me as I exited my practice. "I see all these foreign athletes visiting you for treatment," he said. "Can I tell you, you must be doing something very right or you are fooling the bloody lot of them." He made me think. Success in anything in life is probably down to 50 per cent of what you've got and 50 per cent of what people think you have got. Perceptions create reality.

Irrespective of what treatment protocol is employed, perhaps the most important requirement for healing is a relationship between patient and therapist whereby the patient has total trust and confidence in the therapist. This human element cannot be underestimated. Healing takes place the moment the patient fully believes and trusts the practitioner. Doubt creates a blockage, in terms of healing in the mind and at a cellular level. Belief creates a flow of healing. The mind is such a powerful force in terms of healing that, while a therapist must

---

[3] From the article "Healing Hands" by Conor O'Hagan, *Irish Runner*, vol. 13, no. 3.

never mislead a patient, persuasiveness as an ingredient in treating injury can be effective.

It is well recognised that athletes who think positively and are motivated to do as well as possible in their life and rehabilitation recover more quickly than those with a pessimistic or negative outlook. There are other tools, of course: imagination, creating positive pictures of healing in the mind and repeating affirmations that the injury or illness is healing. These are inner healing aids that all work.

Research using imagery and relaxation on medically incurable cancer patients demonstrated that 41 per cent of patients showed improvement, with 22 per cent showing total remission and 19 per cent tumour regression. Research has proposed three kinds of imagery that can be used for rehabilitation. First and most effective, healing imagery involves you seeing and feeling the injured part getting better. Second, physiotherapy imagery involves imagining the treatment working, for example, the physio's deep friction therapy realigning the scar tissue, or the rehab exercises making the muscles bigger, stronger and more functional. Third, performance imagery, involving the patient imagining the experience and sensations of becoming more physically active or returning fully to playing or competition, provides a motivational edge.

Spirituality is also powerful. I define spirituality as an inner sense of something greater than oneself and recognition of a meaning to existence. Spirituality connects us to our deepest values, beliefs and feelings. It gives meaning and purpose to our lives and affects not just the way we feel, but how we cope with adversity, injury, illness, death and also what lifestyle choices we make. Great champions are balanced in mind, body and spirit. Irrespective of race or religious denomination, all great athletes call upon their beliefs and feelings. Prayer and meditation are an integral part of their success.

Minutes before athletes step out onto the track at the Olympic Games, they go into what is known as the "call room", where they wait to be summoned to the start line for what may be the most important race of their lives. I have worked at five Olympic Games, and my impression of the call room is a place where I have witnessed some of the giants of sport humbled and silenced by tension, stress, fear and anticipation in their final waiting moments. Athletes always feel better when the race gets going, because those minutes waiting in a confined room, with the strong smell of liniment and the razor sharp tension, can be painfully and often detrimentally long.

In a place so quiet – yet full of coiled energy – I tend to the final needs of the athlete and observe every movement. Be they African, European or Asian, the majority of athletes spend those final moments before the race in prayer in request for the perfect performance. I know that if I were taken into a call room and told that I had only minutes to live, my final request would be to get down on my knees to pray for forgiveness and to give thanks.

When the best athletes in the world are injured or ill, they draw on their spirituality and pray to their God. When they win, they give thanks.

When Ronnie Delany won the Olympic 1,500 metres in 1956, he immediately fell onto the track in thanksgiving, praying and proudly sharing his faith with the world. When Noureddine Morceli of Algeria won the 1,500 metres 40 years later, in 1996, he too knelt down on the track in thanksgiving prayer.

We all know how to pray in our hour of need, but it is vital to pray in thanksgiving for the many talents, gifts and blessings bestowed on us. When Portugal's Fernanda Ribeiro, the Olympic gold medal winner in the 10,000 metres in Atlanta in 1996, visited me for treatment in 1998, she was delighted to see I had a statue of Our Lady of Fatima in my clinic. She explained to me that, after she won her Olympic gold medal, she returned to her home in Portugal and walked the 207 kilometres from her village to the Our Lady of Fatima shrine in Fatima in prayer and thanksgiving.

As a physical therapist, I am regularly confronted with debilitating musculoskeletal injuries, some sidelining athletes for years and others threatening careers and livelihoods. Healing has to take place from within. Numerous international scientific studies have identified the therapeutic value of prayer. It is also recognised that "non-local healing" – a healing induced by others praying for the sick or the injured – positively works. The idea that you can transfer healing energy through prayer or through faith is, in my opinion, very real, especially where the recipient has genuine belief.

When the sportsperson puts their trust and belief in me, they unburden themselves of their troubles and hand over the responsibility to me. When I had my own injury troubles as a young teenager, I had a poem that I wrote into my training diary at the start of every year. It was very simple, but it gave me great strength. I hand out the same poem to many of the injured athletes. Written words are powerful, but spoken words are more so. Sometimes an injured athlete only needs a word of encouragement to hang on to.

Don't Quit

When things go wrong, as they sometimes will,
When the road you're trudging seems all uphill,
When the funds are low and the debts are high,
And you want to smile, but you have to sigh,
When care is pressing you down a bit,
Rest if you must, but don't you quit.

Life is queer with its twists and turns,
As every one of us sometimes learns,
And many a fellow turns about,
When he might have won had he stuck it out;
Don't give up though the pace seems slow –
You may succeed with another blow.

Often the goal is nearer than
It seems to a faint and faltering man,
Often the struggler has given up,
When he might have captured the victor's cup
And he learned too late when the night came down,
How close he was to the golden crown.

Success is failure turned inside out –
The silver tint of the clouds of doubt,
And you never can tell how close you are.
It may be near when it seems afar,
So stick to the fight when you're hardest hit –
It's when things seem worst that you mustn't quit.

(*Author unknown*)

So often I've experienced situations firsthand where the best sports-people overcame adversity. The story that stands out for me is that of Kelly Holmes. It's one that any injured sportsperson should know.

When Kelly Holmes was sent to me by UK Athletics in 1998, it was one of those last-hope visits. She had good athletic talent in the early 1990s, but then year after year she got various career-threatening injuries. When she attended my clinic for the first time in 1998, she had torn her Achilles tendon, and was hobbling when walking, never mind running. The Achilles tendon is the curse of many a great athlete and has forced some of the finest talents into an early retirement. Kelly Holmes' visit to Limerick was scheduled for ten days to fully avail of my expertise. The ten-day visit lasted six weeks, and she regularly visited me thereafter for six years. In 1999, Kelly was back racing, although well below international level.

The Olympic year in 2000 was to put her to the test. She trained on the cinder river path along Plassey by the Shannon River, doing 400-metre interval runs because I did not want her training on the synthetic track. She was race rusty coming into the track season, and then came her worst nightmare: she tore her right calf. It was not just any tear. It was a massive twelve-centimetre tear, and the orthopaedic specialist who examined the MRI and Kelly's leg explained to her that it would take twelve to fourteen weeks to heal. The UK Olympic Trials were on in nine weeks, so medically she had no chance. But Kelly Holmes had read the poem "Don't Quit" and she had an inner belief that her body could heal. It was a challenge I was only too excited about.

Two to three times each day, I treated Kelly. Progress was slow, and the UK Trials drew nearer. Three weeks beforehand, Kelly resumed light running, and the following week she improved more. Then she had a test track session of 4 x 400 metres on the University of Limerick track. Kelly huffed and puffed, but completed it. On the Thursday before the trial, which was set for the Saturday, Kelly was dejected. She was back running but was far from race ready; she needed a qualifying time of sub two minutes for 800 metres, yet there was little hope of that. I convinced Kelly to run in the trial, and after much arguing she agreed. We travelled together to Birmingham and it was pure sports psychology that got her to the starting line. She won the UK 800-metre championship in two minutes and four seconds, but was well off the required qualifying mark.

It was six weeks to the Olympic Games in Sydney – what option had she? The Olympic Games only come around every four years. Time waits for nobody, and there was no way the date could be changed. I rang various people in the UK Athletics and British Olympic Association and tried to convince the authorities to give Kelly a special chance. She deserved that. Rules are there for a reason, but they can be bent. Kelly penned a letter to UK Athletics where she outlined that she was slowly getting back to form through training and treatment and asked to be given a chance to be included in the Olympic team.

As it turned out, Kelly Holmes was given a late selection for the Olympic Games in Sydney 2000. It was one of my most memorable moments in sport to witness Kelly, who had struggled so much, fighting her way onto the Great Britain Olympic team, and then, with true Olympic spirit, running to achieve a bronze medal in the 800-metre final.

It was a true argument for never underestimating someone's drive, talent and determination. A few months before the Olympic Games, UK Athletics refused to pay Kelly's medical expenses, stating to me that she was a bottomless pit, costing the system way too much money, and she would be best off retiring. Satisfaction does not come any better than working with someone through adversity, and being part of their achievement by assisting them to overcome injury and go on to win a medal in the Olympic Games.

Even more satisfying is the appreciation that can follow, such as a hand-written letter from an athlete who you have put your heart and soul into helping. The following letter from Kelly Holmes is a special one, and it is framed and displayed in my clinic at the University of Limerick's Sports Arena:

Dear Gerard,

There are few people in this world that I would thank for everything they have done to make me the athlete I am and the one I strive to be. But I thank you for all the time, care and attention you've given to enable me to continue to pursue my goals and dreams.

Without you I may not be running anymore. So everything I achieve from now is because of you.

You have given me hope when I've been at my lowest and belief when I am back running, and that is the most important thing you could ever give an athlete.

I am not the first person to give you thanks and I definitely won't be the last, but Gerard you deserve all the praise you get, so from the bottom of my heart.

Thank you,

Always,

Kelly Holmes

Four years later, at the 2004 Olympic Games in Athens, Kelly Holmes proved once again that "Excellence is perseverance in disguise." She won the 800 metres and the 1,500 metres to become double Olympic champion.

In September 2005 Kelly Holmes was back with me in Limerick. The upcoming Commonwealth Games was her target and she was in with me for a two-week tune-up.

During her visit, I introduced Kelly to my good friend Tim O'Brien. Tim operated his own successful PR business across from my clinic in Patrick Street, and he was a sports fanatic, always promoting Limerick as a great sporting venue. He invented the "Sporting Limerick" logo. He convinced one of Limerick's greatest sons, the multimillionaire JP McManus, to fund the County Board and brand the county GAA jerseys with "Sporting Limerick", so that, instead of the Limerick hurling and football teams sporting a commercial endorsement on their playing outfits, they have the "Sporting Limerick" logo.

On the final day of her visit, Kelly had a business meeting with Tim and they both adjourned for lunch together. Tim was not feeling well during the lunch, and in fact all he could muster up was the bare energy to sip some soup. The following days he spent in hospital and his family briefed me on the tragic news. The 63-year-old Tim, who had fought and appeared to beat cancer 8 years earlier, was again struck down with the deadly disease and was given just weeks to live.

Kelly Holmes decided to visit me in Limerick again. She planned to visit Tim in hospital during her stay. On October 21, the day that Kelly arrived into Shannon, Tim O'Brien's race had come to an abrupt and untimely end. Kelly Holmes was genuinely shocked and shaken by his death. Tim O'Brien's life was dominated by sport and the promotion of Limerick as a sporting centre of excellence, and he had made a profound impact on the many athletes and sportspeople whose lives he touched. During his short illness, Kelly had sent regular text messages and cards to Tim urging him to "fight to your last moment".

Tim's death had a huge impact on Kelly, and actually led to her decision to quit athletics. On her visit, I spent time talking through with Kelly all things life and death. I cancelled all my appointments for two full days and Kelly and I spent from morning to night thrashing out the finer points of life.

A couple of weeks after Tim's death, Kelly phoned me and told me she had organised a press conference for the following day. She asked if she could use my name and if I could check with Tim's family if she could talk about the impact Tim had on her decision to quit. The following morning, after a press conference to over sixty journalists, Kelly Holmes, two-time Olympic gold medal winner, contacted me to let me know that she had announced her retirement and that she had told the media that the shock of Tim O'Brien's death had led her to quit while she was on top.

All the British and international media ran headline stories:

> The double Olympic gold medallist Kelly Holmes announced her retirement in London today, stating: "Tim O'Brien's death shook me to pieces. One minute I was having lunch with Tim and he was passionate about sport and now he is dead. It was an eye opener. I have achieved everything in my sporting life and hopefully have a healthy and fulfilling life ahead of me and Tim O'Brien had his life, but suddenly had it taken away from him. It really upset me. Tim caused me to rethink my whole approach to life. His death is the catalyst for my decision to hang up my spikes and retire."

Over the years I have spent many imaginary hours cycling with Laurent Fignon. The two-time Tour de France winner was born exactly six months before me, in 1960, and I had the pleasure to meet him on various occasions. When his best friend and team mate Pascal Jules died in a car accident, Laurent Fignon went into shock and stated: "For years and years I thought of him every day, and I still think of him regularly. But since his funeral I've been unable to visit his grave. I simply don't have the strength. I can't do it. The way life ends is unique in itself, like the end of a little world. Death at 26 years of age is a notion that I find unbearable."

I also found it unbearable to hear the news that Laurent Fignon, one of cycling's truly great champions, succumbed to pancreatic cancer, and died on August 31, 2010, aged just 50. His death and the death of other friends is the catalyst that spurs me to put on my cycling gear and go out into the bleakest of weather, to turn the pedals, not just those of the bike but the pedals of life, while I still have the health and strength to explore my physical self and feel truly alive.

But I'm fortunate, too, in that I get so many reminders from other people equally driven to succeed and get as much as possible out of life. One of those people is Seán Óg Ó hAilpín, who must personify what the GAA is all about. He also personifies brotherly love and the fellowship of sport. He is one of my true friends, but only for an accident that could have taken his life, we would probably never have met.

In June 2001, Seán Óg was driving along in his car when there was a sudden bang – he was involved in a car crash. He lay in a hospital bed, realising that he was a very lucky man to be alive. His right leg had been operated on; his knee cap had been shattered. The orthopaedic surgeon explained that he may never play contact sports again and Seán Óg respectfully nodded his head. He had already won All-Irelands and had many awards, so he reckoned he had achieved a lot.

Then a specialist in Dublin referred him to me. He arrived into the clinic on two crutches, with a knee the size of a balloon and that he couldn't flex even ten degrees. After that visit, Jimmy McEvoy, the faithful backroom member of the Cork hurling squad, drove Seán Óg up to my clinic twice weekly for weeks on end. The doctors knew Seán Óg was an accomplished hurler, but they had no yardstick of his drive. His drive and hunger to overcome his injury went way above doing everything in his power to resolve it. He did everything I asked of him and way more.

Seán Óg, ever the perfectionist, chiselled himself into such shape that, when he was fully rehabilitated, he was as fine an athlete as any Olympian I ever worked with. Seán Óg was a duel player at the time of his accident, playing both football and hurling at the highest level. His kicking leg for football was his right leg, the injured leg. I explained to Seán Óg the concept of "want all, lose all". He could not have everything. Something had to go. Seán Óg, ever the respectful gentleman, nodded his head and commented: "I know what you are going to say – football must go."

I didn't have to explain myself or say another word. From that moment, hurling was his mission. Some sportspeople focus too much on their little niggles and injuries, and rob themselves of their true potential. Not Seán Óg. He said: "Let's drive on." The effort and work that he put himself through to get back to the top was, to this day, by far the best I have ever witnessed in an amateur sportsman.

On a later occasion, when putting Ronan O'Gara, Seán Óg and Setanta Ó hAilpín through a specially designed conditioning session, Seán Óg buckled the two professional sportsmen and had them wondering what material he was made of. In 2004, when the final whistle was blown on Cork's victory in the All-Ireland hurling final in Croke Park, Seán Óg Ó hAilpín looked up to the Heavens and thanked his Lord and lucky star. The great Kilkenny hurler Henry Shefflin shook his hand in congratulations, and beckoned to swap jerseys. Seán Óg politely replied: "Sorry, Henry, it's being kept for a special man in Limerick."

Seán Óg had faced his demons. He and his team were All-Ireland champions once again, and he was awarded with the Hurler of the Year award and named Cork captain for the following year. As a true measure of the man he is, weeks after the All-Ireland, Seán Óg drove to Limerick and presented me with the jersey he wore in the All-Ireland final, with the message across it; "Gerard, thanks for the belief. Seán Óg Ó hAilpín, Hurler of the Year 2004." He was spot-on: belief is paramount to success.

When Seán Óg's younger brother Setanta Ó hAilpín broke onto the Cork senior hurling scene, the GAA world knew it had a new star in the making. Surely he was wasted on the indigenous amateur game of Irish hurling? That summer season of Sundays in 2003, he was sensational on the field along with being the heart throb of every young lady in the country.

When he visited my clinic for tune-ups, I marvelled at his physical capabilities and had no option but to encourage him to spread his wings and fly away to follow his dream of becoming a professional athlete. He signed up with Carlton Football Club in Melbourne, Australia and, as a rookie, he adapted straightaway to being a full-time professional athlete.

So much hope, so much promise and expectation, along with the demands of having to perform every time he togged out and a conflict with his Melbourne club manager, threw him into despair and he touched the darkness of depression. He was full of anger and frustration, lashing out at everyone and anyone. I had to bite my lip and listen to him venting his anger several times on long-distance phone calls. I just listened; I was the ear he needed to cope with his turmoil. Sometimes just listening and giving a few practical tips is all that is required.

Months later, when Setanta had settled and found his form again, he came to visit me in Limerick. He grabbed me – or rather bear-hugged me – almost squashing me breathless. I've captured the moment in my mind and it's worth a thousand words. Then he presented me with his navy Carlton football jersey, signed with a silver pen with the message:

To Ger,

"Short term pain for long-term gain."

Your phone calls changed my life. Thanks so much for the great work you have done for me. I won't forget it. You taught me that those who work hard reap the rewards. Thanks for showing me this.

Setanta Ó hAilpín
#17, Carlton Football Club,
Melbourne, Australia

19

The Rewards of Perseverance – Ronan O'Gara, Séamus Moynihan, Henry Shefflin and John Tennyson

In March of 2005 Ronan O'Gara came knocking at my door. He looked like a man in dire straits. He had injured his right knee playing for Munster against the Gwent Dragons in a Celtic League match at Rodney Parade in Wales. Straightaway, it looked bad: he was carried off the pitch, unable to walk. The Lions Tour that summer looked like it would have to do without him. The feather in his cap of being selected for the Lions Tour would go too, along with the handsome pay cheque.

O'Gara sought the professional expertise of Mr Ray Moran, the specialist knee surgeon in Dublin. The worst was confirmed: he had a grade two tear of the medial collateral ligament, but, worse again, the anterior cruciate ligament was also partially torn. Surgery looked to be the only solution and Mr Moran talked through the prognosis with Ronan. With surgery there was no chance of his making the Lions Tour, then seven weeks away. So Ronan signed a consent form which gave the surgeon license to do whatever repair work he deemed necessary, once he was on the operating table.

Then, the morning of the surgery, Ronan threw Mr Moran a curveball. The Dublin-based physio Alan Kelly had suggested O'Gara consult with me before having surgery in an attempt to get the leg treated and healthy for the Lions Tour, and that he deal with any necessary surgery afterwards. Mr Moran is a good friend of mine, and he contacted me directly to see if I could commit to ensure the necessary result.

O'Gara wrote about his treatment in his autobiography:[4]

For me, the decision to work with Ger was straightforward. I needed massively intensive, one-on-one attention and he was the best in the business. He was my only chance of making the Lions Tour. [...] I was in Ger's clinic five days a week, six hours a day and sometimes we'd do a Saturday session as well. I used to stay with Quinny [Alan Quinlan] in Limerick for three nights during the week and do the 120-mile round journey from Cork on the other days.

The regime was murder. The hardest thing I ever had to do in my career... It was like he took me apart and built me back up again. I went to him with an injured right knee and he identified about five other areas of serious weakness in my physical make-up. My left knee, he said, was weak and unstable. That was my good knee.

There were days in his clinic when I broke down. My body couldn't take it. My mind was making demands that my body couldn't meet. I went through every emotion from hope to despair and back. You spend so much time trying to push through the pain barrier that it wrecks your head and drains your body. One of Ger's partners is a Kerryman Ger Keane and he was incredibly positive. When things were getting on top of me he kept me going. [...]

Before I left Ger's clinic he had me doing one-legged hops, jumping off small tables and all kinds of exercises. I knew it was all right. I felt like a new man.

O'Gara, in fact, started in the Celtic Cup Final against Llanelli seven weeks after his injury occurred. He was already back to his best:

The match went like a dream. We [Munster] won. I scored 17 points, including an early try, and got the Man of the Match award. I felt fresh, strong and sharper than I had felt in about three years. [...] After all the additional work that Ger had done I had about an extra 5 metres on my pass off either hand... I was pretty euphoric in a television interview afterwards and I didn't hold back in my praise of Ger... Until you have experienced a serious injury you have no idea how lonely and challenging it can be. I was over that now.

With some injuries, time heals and the doctor sends the bill; others need a lot of work and commitment. As a physical therapist, the challenge

---

[4] *Ronan O'Gara: My Autobiography*, Dublin: Transworld Ireland, 2009, Chapter 14.

is always there to expedite injury time, to help athletes cope through their crisis – but the task is also to educate them and give them hope, and facilitate the healing process in both mind and body.

In July 2005, Kerry football manager Jack O'Connor sent Séamus Moynihan to me in an effort to have him healthy for the All-Ireland semi-final and, hopefully, the final that September. Jack O'Connor knew that if he ever needed a man to go to war with, Séamus Moynihan would be on the top of his list. Since making his intercounty debut with Kerry in 1992, fourteen seasons earlier, Séamus had become a living legend in the world of Gaelic football. Séamus could play at wing-back, centre-back or full-back and perform to such a high level in each that you'd think whatever position you saw him play in on a particular day was his best. He had a style and panache that were uniquely his and those dashing incisive runs from half-back through opposing defences worked magic when he was healthy and on form.

My best effort to rid Séamus of his back and hip injury was good enough that Jack and his selectors named Séamus on the starting team for the All-Ireland. But on the day of the final the great player was not firing on all cylinders and he was later substituted. Head held low, he walked into the tunnel under the Croke Park stands. The pangs of disappointment and frustration brought him to tears. Not tears of self-pity, but tears for failing to deliver. He had let himself and his people down. This was completely new territory for him. In his lengthy career with Kerry there had been lean years, years when Kerry saw no silver-ware coming home – but to be taken off for underperforming in an All-Ireland final in Croke Park, against great rivals Tyrone, was too hard to stomach; perhaps harder still because the men from across the border won the final.

Séamus ploughed on into the winter season, playing with his local club Glenflesk, but the injury nearly sent him demented and he confided in his long-time friend Fr Kevin O'Sullivan that he would hang up his intercounty boots and slip out of playing for his county, hoping that it would go unnoticed.

Fr Kevin knew that if Séamus were to retire on an injury, in defeat, then he would come to regret it years later. He urged Séamus to come to me. On the first week of November 2005, my colleague Ger Keane and I met with Séamus in my clinic in Limerick and put together a rehabilitation and performance strategy for a six-month individualised programme. This was designed to get Séamus healthy for the following championship year. It involved visits to the clinic every two weeks for three hours of intensive physio and intensive rehabilitation sessions, and a home exercise programme of 90 minutes every day, along with cycling and pool work to build endurance and cardiovascular fitness. The long, hard grind and slow progress of the winter began to yield results in the spring, and when the summer arrived Séamus Moynihan had a new-found spring in his step. Not only was he more flexible, but his core was the strongest it had ever been.

At 34 years of age he had found a new gear and he was injury free for the first season in several years. Séamus was Man of the Match in several games that summer, and he played one of the best games of his career in the 2006 All-Ireland final when Kerry won easily against an underperforming Mayo. Ger Keane and I sat in Croke Park that day, joyous that we had contributed to seeing Séamus Moynihan play his last intercounty match and end his career at the very top. To see him hold the Sam Maguire cup, which he and his Kerry team mates won, brought tears to our eyes.

On the Wednesday after the final, we shared a special evening in Séamus' house, along with his wife Noreen and newborn son Jamie. This great player, respecting that every sportsperson has his day, announced to us in the privacy of his home that fifteen years in the green and gold jersey of Kerry, serving his county, had been enough. Family and playing for the local club would be his lifeline for the years ahead. Sometimes the hardest decision for an athlete to make is to retire at the top of their game, but Séamus had made the right choice, and had walked away entirely content and with no regrets. That's a privilege few athletes get to enjoy, but he had deserved it.

A few weeks later, ever the gentleman, Séamus presented me with his Kerry jersey and Adidas boots that he wore in the All-Ireland final, with the written message:

Ger,

The dream was always running ahead of me. To catch up, to live for a moment in unison with it, that was a miracle! Thanks for making 2006 so special.

Séamus Moynihan

On January 19, 2007, I was invited to a celebration of the football career of Séamus Moynihan, held at the Great Southern Hotel in Killarney and organised by his own club, Glenflesk. Over 600 people attended the dinner function, and Mícheál O'Muircheartaigh, Ogie Moran and I were asked to speak a few words of wisdom and insight about Seamus.

Aside from acknowledging that Séamus epitomised what is best about Gaelic football, I mentioned that the occasion epitomised the importance of the local hero, and the power of the local club and the parish.

It is obvious to me that international sports stars who are household names may make their name, fame and fortune on the sports grounds and tracks around the world, and they are respected for their achievements, but the GAA club player, the inter-county player, is connected to his local club and the sporting heritage and prowess of his county, and is ultimately connected to his own people, young and old. In Séamus Moynihan's case, the celebration of his football career was presented by his people, reflecting their local pride and that his success was their success. An accolade is much more powerful when celebrated by one's very own community of family, friends and neighbours, and extended parish and sporting community.

In August 2010, Kilkenny hurling manager Brian Cody contacted me. Along with his backroom medical staff, he put it to me to take their two star players, both with acute cruciate ligament injuries, for treatment. This was just four weeks before the All-Ireland final where Kilkenny were shooting for the historic five-in-a-row. Henry Shefflin and John Tennyson had both succumbed to the dreaded injury just weeks before the biggest day of their lives, the day when the "drive for five" could reward them with a historical victory. For Shefflin it was actually the second time he'd sustained the injury, as he tore the cruciate in his other knee in 2007.

The odds of recovering in time were stacked against them, but they had the belief, and also the dedication, commitment, drive, work ethic and ability to endure pain. Eleven days before the All-Ireland final, Shefflin and Tennyson both turned up in Nowlan Park for training. Team players were shocked to see them and those watching from the stand reacted like they'd seen Lazarus rise from the dead. Around 8,000 people flooded into Nowlan Park to witness the spectacle. Mobile camera phones were flashing galore. Fans were on their phones, texting and phoning their friends and family with the news. The miracle of all miracles had occurred. Shefflin was on fire, jumping into the air for the high balls and driving them into the back of the net. Likewise, Tennyson was defending as good as new. Kilkenny would be sure of the victory now. The GAA media went into overdrive.

What made their comeback against the odds happen was their belief, along with all the other necessary components of success. However, it rained heavily on the day of the final and the pitch at Croke Park had turned slippery. The fact that it hadn't rained in over three weeks added to the perils of the surface. Henry Shefflin got off to a fierce start, playing faster than ever. Then he jumped for a high ball and, on landing, badly twisted his leg. With that, his day was done. He hobbled off the pitch in agony, damaging cartilage in his knee. He had lasted until fourteen minutes into the game. Tennyson played on for the full 70 minutes; his knee held up. But it just wasn't to be Kilkenny's day. They had come up against a Tipperary team that peaked brilliantly on the day, with Larry Corbett scoring three magnificent goals to help ensure Tipperary were All-Ireland hurling champions once again. It had been a nine-year wait since their previous win in 2001, another lesson perhaps that, in sport, it can be a feast or a famine. But the lesson that day for Shefflin was that luck is always a factor too, and one we have no control over.

But setbacks come and go; talent and genius remain. Nine months after that All-Ireland defeat, Henry Shefflin was back to his brilliant best, scoring 1-9 in the Leinster final against Dublin. Some people had wondered if Shefflin would ever be the same player again, and if he had been wise to play in the All-Ireland final in 2010 – that perhaps he did himself some permanent damage. His performance in that Leinster final was the answer. Shefflin was as electrifying as ever, as Kilkenny won their seventh Leinster title in succession and Shefflin himself collected his twelfth Leinster medal. There wasn't even a minor hint of the knee injury that cut short his season in 2010.

In 2011 Shefflin reached the peak of his sporting career when he won his eighth All-Ireland Championship medal, a record that he shares with the most eminent hurlers in the history of the game, including Christy Ring of Cork and John Doyle of Tipperary. Persistence and determination had once again paid off.

20

The Great African Athletes

Some people are like magpies, always sitting on the fence. Others are like beavers, always on the go, making things happen. From a young age I learned the lesson that if you want a job done ask a busy man. If you want something done right, go to the top man, the boss.

In 1978, when I was sixteen years of age and in boarding school at the Salesian College in Pallaskenry, Co. Limerick, there were Trocáire boxes on each of the dining tables in the students' refectory during Lent. They sat there week after week, with none of us touching them, and one day it dawned on me: sure, as students, we were all broke. We didn't have any money other than coppers to put into the boxes. It was the parents who had the money.

We were all well aware of the famine, poverty and drought in Biafra in those years, and the pictures on television struck a note with me. Salesian College also had an Agriculture College attached to the second-ary boarding school, and the food on the students' tables was fit for a king. It was a far cry from the stricken poverty of Africa. I felt I needed to do something to help. There were over 400 students, teachers and staff between the 2 schools. I reasoned that if I did something purpose-ful, and had each person sponsor me just £1, then I would generate over £400 for the Trocáire fund.

I went to the headmaster and told him I wanted to run from the college to the Town Hall in Limerick City and out again – over 25 miles in total. This would be my way to raise some funds. The headmaster was sceptical but after some further convincing he agreed. I drew up a big poster, with the sign "Marathon Run by Gerard Hartmann in aid of

Trocáire. Please pledge £1." The students weren't too bothered about putting their coins into a Lenten box, but if a fellow student was doing something meaningful for their money, I knew they would support it.

Running long distances like that was still something of an unknown in 1979: the running boom had not begun. Running a marathon was looked upon as being a bit like going to the moon, especially for a seventeen-year-old. Fundraising and sponsorship to do such events had not yet caught on, but it had caught the interest of the school that Sunday in 1979, when the headmaster, rector and students gathered to cheer me on my way. It was a big occasion for the school, one of their own students running all the way into Limerick and back out. Fr Martin Loftus, our wonderful sports master, patiently drove in his car behind me, tracking my every step. In the end, more than £400 was raised.

Little did I think on that day that over fourteen years later my work as a physical therapist would bring me into contact with the great African athletes, many of whom had grown up in abject poverty. I would establish my own clinic, the Hartmann International Sports Injury Clinic, high up above the Great Rift Valley in the village of Iten, Kenya, where over 600 of the world's best runners live and train some 8,500 feet above sea level. The Kenyan people have influenced and impressed me so much.

Two such Kenyan greats Moses Kiptanui and William Tanui burst onto the international athletics stage in 1992, the same year I started making a reputation for myself within the world of athletics as "the Irish physio with the magic hands". Moses Kiptanui won the world junior 1,500-metre title in 1990, and from 1992 to 1998 he set over a dozen world records in events ranging from the 3,000 metres to the 3,000 metres steeplechase and the 5,000 metres. So, when I am asked about the greatest athlete I ever worked with, I typically respond with the name Moses Kiptanui. Such was his ability that he purposely shaved fractions of a second off his record times to ensure he achieved a new world record, and he pocketed the record bonus and International Association of Athletics Federations (IAAF) Golden League gold bars into the bargain.

I have never witnessed an athlete run with such rhythm and grace as Kiptanui did. Perhaps I have some bias towards the 3,000 metre steeplechase, as I had won a national underage title in the event in 1979.

Like poetry in motion, Kiptanui hurdled the 28 steeplechase barriers and 7 water jumps in this most arduous of track events to become the first man in history to break the 8-minute barrier. We remain lifelong friends and share that special bond that sport can bring.

William Tanui ("Big William") won the 800-metre gold medal at the 1992 Olympic Games in Barcelona and on visits to Kenya I regularly meet him. On a recent meeting, I was saddened to hear his story that his house had been burgled and his Olympic gold medal had been taken.

Another of the great Kenyan athletes I have had the pleasure of meeting is the father of my good friend Martin Keino, and the first Kenyan to make a major sporting impact, winning a gold medal in the 1,500 metres at the 1968 Mexico Olympics and a gold medal in the 3,000-metre steeplechase at the 1972 Munich Olympics. His name is Kip Keino, and he is also known as the father of Kenyan distance running.

Kip grew up in the impoverished outskirts of Eldoret in western Kenya, in a little village named Kipsamo. He was one of six children, and was reared in a mud hut. No one could ever have imagined that a young boy from such a poor background would make such an impact on both the athletic and humanitarian world.

The future was bleak in Kenya in the early 1960s and one lived either in extreme poverty or was lucky enough to be enlisted in the Kenyan Armed Forces or Police Force. When Kip joined the police force at eighteen years of age, his life was to change: he was introduced to competitive running, and with the success he achieved at Olympic level he earned worldwide respect. To this day, he is regarded as arguably the greatest of all the Kenyan runners.

The impact of his success spurred a running boom in his country, and so many young boys and girls have followed in Kip's footsteps to become world and Olympic champions. They have seen that, through running, there is an opportunity and a way out of extreme poverty.

In 1963, when Kip Keino was on police duty, he stumbled upon two emaciated children. They had been abandoned. Their hunger was so great that they were eating dirt by the roadside. The local authorities gave Kip permission to care for the children, and that was the start of Kip's real calling from God. As well as being credited as father of the Kenyan running revolution, he is recognised as father of his nation in a much more meaningful context than athletics.

Kip and his wife Phyllis are currently parents to over 100 children, all orphans, who live on the Keino farm near Eldoret. In the past 30 years Kip and Phyllis have reared over 2,000 children. Their 200-acre farm Kazi Mingi – which in Swahili means "hard work" – employs 22 staff. They take in babies who have been thrown out by their parents. Many are AIDs orphans and their mothers are prostitutes who either can't or don't want to raise the children. They have been rescued from public toilets, dustbins, the roadside and the bushes. Kip collects them and takes them to the orphanage, where Phyllis and the care workers look after and rear the children.

When I visited the orphanage, Kip was proud to point out that, of the thousands of orphans he has reared, some have gone on to become doctors, nurses, university lecturers, teachers; others own their own businesses. They all received an upbringing, an education and a quality of life they would never have encountered without the Keinos.

Kip now also chairs the National Olympic Committee of Kenya, and has received funding for the orphanage from the Kenyan Government. He has used his world contacts to receive support from the International Olympic Committee, from the car company Daimler-Chrysler, and also Oxfam and the Rotary Club. Kip and Phyllis live modestly, but work endless hours tirelessly. Kip found something purposeful and meaningful away from the spotlight and glory of the Olympic stadium. He found his true calling. He and Phyllis are on an obvious God-given mission.

The Keinos have recently completed a school which caters for 800 children. Kip is often consulted and respected by all members of Kenyan society. I met Kip only a number of years ago in London. He was there to run the London Marathon. His finishing time was 4 hours and 30 minutes – well over 2 hours slower than the winner, but the reward for him was the £150,000 he raised for Oxfam. Kip recalled that when he was a toddler it was Oxfam who put a well in his village, and without that he may never have been healthy enough to have become an athlete.

It can't be overstated that Kip Keino has made a tremendous impact on the world. The memories of his awesome athletic achievements pale in comparison to the achievements he has accomplished off the track. He is a true winner in sport, but also in life – and further testimony that, through sport and hard work, great things can be achieved.

I have worked with upwards of 300 of the top Kenyan athletes, many of whom are my lifelong friends: Moses Kiptanui, William Tanui, Daniel Komen, Benjamin Limo and Moses Masai are just some. Of course, there is also my "twin brother" Douglas Wakiihuri; he calls my mother "Mum" and often phones her up for a regular chat.

Douglas was always different. He was born and raised in Mombasa, at sea level, which proves that you don't have to be born or train at altitude to make it to the top in distance running. At eighteen years of age, Douglas was not a good runner by Kenyan standards, but he had heart. He wrote to the famous coach in Japan, Mr Nakamura, who coached the famous marathon runner Toshihiko Seko. Douglas pleaded with Mr Nakamura to bring him to Japan and that he would work for his keep. The rest is distance-running history.

Four years after arriving in Japan, Douglas Wakiihuri won Kenya's first-ever gold medal in the marathon when he won the World Championships in 1987 in Rome. The following year, at the Olympic Games in Seoul, he won the silver medal, being out-foxed at the finish by the Italian Gelindo Bordin. Douglas went on to dominate marathon running for a few years after, winning the London and New York marathons before a career-threatening knee injury knocked him back. It was then our brotherhood relationship began. Douglas lived with me in my home in Gainesville, Florida for three years. I not only addressed his knee injury but coached him to winning the IAAF World Cup Marathon in Athens in 1995.

Many years later, the great memory man of RTÉ sport Jimmy McGee visited my clinic and museum at the University of Limerick and we reminisced on triathlon and Ironman times of old. Then I hit Jimmy with the quiz question: "Who won the silver medal in the 1984 Los Angeles Olympic Marathon?" Jimmy responded, "Indeed, it was our very own John Treacy."

"Now, Jimmy", I asked, "who won the Olympic marathon silver medal in the following Olympics in Seoul in 1988 and where is that medal now?"

True to his memory, he replied, "The great Douglas Wakiihuri, from Kenya, won the Olympic silver, and I assume he has it in his home in Nairobi."

"No, Jimmy," I said. "Look into the glass case here." I pointed out Sonia O'Sullivan's Olympic silver medal on display, and Jim Hogan's European Marathon gold medal from 1966 in Budapest. Jim Cregan competed for Ireland in previous Olympics but became so disgruntled with the Irish Athletics Federation that he changed his name to Hogan and ran for England, winning the European Marathon.

I showed him Marcus O'Sullivan's three gold medals from the World Indoor Championships, which were sitting alongside Frank O'Mara's two world indoors gold medals won for the 3,000 metres. And there at the rear of the display case in the purple velvet box with the insignia "Seoul Olympic Games" was the Olympic Marathon silver medal from Seoul in 1988.

"My goodness!" said Jimmy, "I never knew we had two Olympic silver marathon medals from successive Olympics here in Ireland. Tell me, how and why is it here?"

"Friendship," I replied, "and the fellowship of sport are a powerful combination."

It was in Nairobi, Kenya, days before I travelled to Macau for the Great Britain Olympic Team training camp for the Beijing Games, that Douglas Wakiihuri, Lornah Kiplagat, Ger Keane and I shared a wonderful meal together, where the talk was speckled with the beginnings of Olympic anticipation. It was one of those nights that will stay animated in my mind as we shared stories of the Olympic exploits of some of our great friends. That same night, Douglas had an extraordinary grin on his face. He was like a young boy bursting with excitement but holding back from telling us something. The following morning, at 6.00 a.m., he was unexpectedly waiting at Kenyatta International Airport as we were due to depart. He had come to say goodbye and, after handing me a small packet, he looked me in the eye, gave me a long embrace and said, "Daktari Gerard, take good care of yourself, and don't open this package until you arrive in Ireland. It's my surprise for you."

I opened it as I waited at the luggage carousel in Cork Airport. Ger Keane watched me carefully tear back the brown paper wrapping to see a dusty purple velvet box. Inside was Douglas Wakiihuri's Olympic silver medal, which he had won in the 1988 Seoul Olympic Marathon, surely the most prized possession of his sporting life. A neat handwritten note folded in the box read:

> Daktari Gerard, every medal has a bright shiny side which everybody sees, but also a dark side which lies in its shadow. I give you this medal as a gift of our friendship to put in your clinic so that everybody who sees it may be inspired and touched by its success and so allowing it to shine brightly forever more.
>
> Your twin brother,
>
> Wakiihuri

On May 17, 2007, the day that Ronnie Delany officially opened my new clinic and launched the Hartmann Collection – a museum of international sporting memorabilia at the University Sports Arena at the University of Limerick – Douglas Wakiihuri requested that the following message be read out:

> Ladies and Gentlemen,
>
> I, Douglas Wakiihuri from Kenya, would like to take this opportunity to congratulate you all on this special occasion to this great nation of Ireland.
>
> This is my dream as it is yours, too, and for many more dreams to be fulfilled. Let the light shine on to the young and the great and to all who cheer us all the way. To those who pray for us and to our families who encourage and believe beyond no doubt that we are all together at the finish line.
>
> I would like to thank you Mr Gerard Hartmann and all who have made this place the Hartmann Clinic and Museum a special place, a golden dream come true. Mr Hartmann you are a miracle that has been part of my life to be remembered now and forever.
>
> Love to Mum. Thank you very much.
>
> Douglas Wakiihuri

Joseph Ebuya was a young man with no future, nothing to dream of. He lived homeless on the streets in the rural poverty-stricken town of Nyahururu, Kenya. His daily existence consisted of searching through rubbish bins for food to stave off the hunger pangs and stay alive.

Occasionally he watched a group of light-footed elite Kenyan runners pass by. One day he decided to run behind them. He was barefoot, but it felt good to be running after the well-clad runners. He joined in again and again, and one day one of the athletes gave him a pair of old used shoes.

Each day he waited at the side of the road and when the group of athletes came by he joined in. He had no home; he'd never gone to school – but now he felt a sense of purpose joining a group of top athletes who, in their unspoken way, seemed to respect him. Joseph had never felt respect before. Within two years, Joseph was competing internationally and, in 2010, he won the world cross country title.

The Kenyan runners often take their success in sport and use it towards a greater cause, beyond sport. Take another of my good friends, Lornah Kiplagat, who won the world cross country title and three world half marathon titles. It is at Lornah's High Altitude Training Centre that my clinic in Iten, Kenya is based.

Lornah Kiplagat also runs a foundation for poor girls to educate and prepare them to take the SAT exams in order to gain entry to US universities. She selects 30 girls every year, from the poorest backgrounds, who have done well in their schooling. Twelve professors visit her training centre for twelve weeks each summer to educate and prepare the girls to take the SAT test to go on scholarship to universities like Harvard, Stanford, MIT and other top-end universities. Lornah Kiplagat had recognised that boys get nearly all the opportunities in Kenya. She wanted to change that, to give women a chance, and she realised that education was the best place to start.

Lornah Kiplagat thinks big. She believes that some day one of her students will become the first woman president of Kenya. She follows the motto: "If you shoot for the moon, at least if you don't reach it you will fall among the stars."

What inspires and moves me most about the Kenyan athletes is their humanity, their Christianity and their genuine respect for self and humankind. The great Sally Barsosio, who at the age of 22 won the 10,000 metres at the World Championships in 1997, once wrote me this note:

Daktari Gerard,

Thanks a lot for treating me which led me to a gold medal in 1997. I am back again to you and I hope to go for gold after your help again.

May God bless your efforts with the work of your hands.

Thanks a lot and may He lead you to live 120 years, to lead his people including me to do wonderful things on earth.

Daktari, you mean so much in the world of sports and everybody will live to know and remember you even unborn ones.

Thanks for being loving and caring to every sportsperson. May God bless you and lead you throughout your life.

Big love,

Sally Barsosio

Vivian Cheruiyot won the World Championship 5,000 metres in Berlin in 2009 with a brilliant performance. She then went on to show that she is the best female distance runner in the world by winning the world cross country title in 2011, and the world 5,000 and 10,000 metres in Daegu, South Korea, also in 2011. Yet Vivian is barely 5 feet tall and weighs only 89 pounds. In fact, she's so light and small looking that one could assume that a puff of wind would blow her away.

So where do these super-lightweight runners get their extraordinary strength from? It cannot be all physical. I strongly believe that it is will-power and Christian belief on top of drive and an enormous work ethic that gives them the competitive edge. Inner belief is so important. At times, I think it is the most important ingredient.

When Vivian came to me for treatment in 2010 she shared her spirit and sporting fellowship with everyone she came in contact with in Ireland. Injured, but undeterred, she travelled down to Castleisland in Kerry with my colleague Ger Keane. While there, she quickly became the life and soul of the local athletics club. In fact, she was made life member of the Gneeveguilla Athletics Club; perhaps, if it were possible, we could extend Irish citizenship to her. It's now 55 years since Ronnie Delany won Ireland's last Olympic gold medal on the athletic track, and it could be that and more before Ireland wins another, unless some very unique talent emerges from our gene pool. Otherwise, perhaps we had better import.

In my days as an athlete and triathlete, training and competing in triathlons around the world, I thought that my competitive sporting life was my only life. But I would have fallen off the bike if I had been told what the years after triathlon would hold for me. The career experiences I have enjoyed in the years since go way beyond anything I ever dreamed of or imagined. It is because of this that I am sure that what happens in our lives is all part of destiny, part of a greater plan that God has for us. When I meet people who are down and out, who are suffering because things have gone wrong, I tell them my story. I tell them how my accident and broken hip initially made me so low, and yet eventually it all came right. Sometimes we can never imagine the greater world waiting for us. Sometimes, like heaven, it has to be believed to be seen.

21

The Secrets of Success in Sport and in Life

Talent almost certainly plays some role in the athlete making it to the top of their sport. But talent is essentially unquantifiable, which is why some people simply refer to it as the "x-factor".

What is certain is that talent comes in many shapes and forms, and I have worked with enough champions to know that talent alone does not ensure success. It's just one of many ingredients necessary to create the sporting champion.

When I first took up running and six years later found myself on an athletic scholarship in America, I was doing something that I was passionate about. I did not know at that stage that my dad was an accomplished sportsman in his day. He had captained the Limerick Rowing Club and once beat the actor Richard Harris to win a Munster Schools Sprint title. Indeed, on October 18, 2003, on the day I was participating in the 25th Anniversary Hawaii Ironman, my dad, Patrick Hartmann, at 73 years of age, participated in the Masters Rowing Regatta on the head of Charles River in Boston, US. The two Hartmann boys were competing in North America on the same day, knowing that we were both born to perform.

I only later learnt that two of my uncles, my mother's brothers, were also top sportsmen. Noel Deasy played intercounty hurling for Clare and was on the team that won the Oireachtas tournament in the 1950s. He once marked the legendary Christy Ring, reportedly keeping him scoreless from play in one great game. His younger brother Mickey Deasy also won two Dr Harty Cups, or Munster colleges hurling titles, and an All-Ireland colleges hurling title, playing for St Flannan's of

Ennis. He also won an All-Ireland Schools 200-metre title. So maybe genes do have a role to play.

Some element of natural or God-given talent will help, and so, of course, will some luck. People might say they are lucky to be such a great athlete or sportsperson because they were simply born with the talent. Talent certainly offers a head start, but the qualities that make successful sportspeople are in fact many. Champions of sport have desire, passion and spirit – and also perseverance, focus and an enthusiasm for what they do. They must also set goals and have a plan, and, most important of all, have a positive approach and believe in themselves. If you investigate any successful sportsperson you will discover that hard work, preparation and dedication, along with commitment and a good support structure, are the key driving forces behind their sporting success. As the great golfer Gary Player famously said, "The harder you work, the luckier you get." I believe luck is simply opportunity meeting preparation.

Many athletes turn out to be "late bloomers". In sports terms, they don't appear to have any talent, at least not at first. When I was sixteen years old and winning races all around Munster, I remember there was a small lad from Cork. He showed up at some of the same races, but he was too small and had no apparent speed to make any impact. Those runners who always finished in the medals felt bad for him because we could see how hard he tried and how determined he was. But he was just developing at a slower rate. His name was Marcus O'Sullivan, and he would turn out to be a multiple world champion.

In 1979, at the Munster Club Championships, a few weeks before heading off on scholarship to the US, I remember winning the 800 metres, the 1,500 metres, the 1,500 metres steeplechase and the 3,000 metres. Marcus O'Sullivan had one of his best runs that day, finishing second to me in the 3,000 metres. Afterwards, we chatted for a bit and he said he envied me getting an athletic scholarship, but because his times were way too slow he never saw himself getting the same chance. Marcus worked in a factory following secondary school, yet he continued to run. No one predicted that he would make it, but at age nineteen he finally made a big breakthrough and, with that, earned himself a scholarship to the famous Villanova University. There he would be coached by the legendary Jumbo Elliott, who was known as "Maker of Milers, Maker of Men", and the man who guided many running greats, including Ireland's Ronnie Delany, Noel Carroll and Eamonn Coghlan.

Marcus O'Sullivan had little obvious athletic talent and, as a youngster, very little speed, yet he reached the top of his sport. His story is proof that one should never underestimate the young athlete who has passion, desire and the will to take something seriously. He persevered and, once his body matured and developed, his natural speed came with it. He went on to set a national record in the 800 metres and competed in four Olympic Games for Ireland in the 1,500 metres. But his greatest achievement was in winning three world indoor titles in the 1,500 metres, in 1987, 1989 and 1993. Marcus is also one of only three people ever to have run over 100 sub-four minute miles, which is an extraordinary feat by any sporting standards.

He is also the first to admit that he was never academically inclined, but when he got to Villanova he applied himself to both his sport and to his studies. The memory of working long shifts on the factory floor in Cork was all the encouragement he needed.

Not only did he go on to receive his Master's in Business Administration from Villanova University, but he is presently the head track and field coach at Villanova, a position he has held for over thirteen years now. In a beautiful twist of fate, Marcus is now responsible himself for mastering young milers and helping athletes maximise their talents in athletics and in life – and I can't imagine anyone better qualified.

When Paula Radcliffe was eleven years old, her dad, Peter, took her down to the local athletic club, Bedford and County Athletics Club. There she met up with over 30 young girls of a similar age, some of whom would become lifelong friends. In her first race, Paula finished second last – not the most auspicious start to any sporting career. Three years later, the Bedford and County girls qualified to compete in the under-15s at the English National Cross Country. Paula made the team, but finished very far down the field in 299th place.

At the club Paula was coached by Alex and Rosemary Staunton, whose own daughter also enjoyed running. By 1992, at age eighteen, Paula had made considerable progress under the Stauntons' guidance and not only won the English junior cross county title, but also won the world junior cross country title, which was staged on a snowy course in Boston. Some athletic experts contended that Paula Radcliffe would not make it at senior level. Their view was that her running style was too ungainly, and that any athlete who nodded their head on each stride as she did was expending way too much energy. They also argued she had little chance of making it at senior level against the all-conquering Kenyan and Ethiopian athletes.

Yet Paula applied herself to her sport with unyielding determination and self-belief. People worldwide would soon be cheering her on because they recognised in this gallant girl someone who was not the swiftest or the most graceful of runners, but who was a workhorse, someone who never gave up. It took Paula nine years to win a first senior world title, and when she won the world cross country title in Ostend, Belgium in 2001, she was one of the most popular winners of the event. Paula went on to run an amazing 2 hours, 15 minutes and 25 seconds for the marathon. She won the New York Marathon three times and also the London Marathon three times, along with the 2005 World Championship Marathon, in Helsinki.

Neither Paula nor Marcus O'Sullivan had obvious athletic talent at the beginning; their talent lay in their ability to persevere, to train hard and to endure pain – and, above all, they shared the desire to succeed and the self-belief to achieve whatever it was they set out to do.

I was both fortunate and privileged to work with Marcus O'Sullivan for the last six years of his running career, and to this day we remain best friends and regularly meet up to share our views and thoughts on human performance.

Paula Radcliffe never gives up believing in herself. I have been working with her for 14 years now, and at 38 years of age she is preparing to toe the starting line in her fifth Olympic Games in London in 2012, once again in the marathon. One has to admire her perseverance as she chases the one championship medal that has eluded her prolific career. An Olympic medal is one that all great athletes strive to win. She will need belief beyond belief to succeed, and plenty of luck.

The world can marvel at the great athletic talent that is visible and obvious: the likes of Carl Lewis, Usain Bolt, Tiger Woods, Earvin "Magic" Johnson and other almost supernatural athletes who will always reach the top in their sport. It is somewhat harder to understand how an athlete who has not got apparent talent or qualifications makes it – sometimes they can be the victim of a sceptic's moan that they have probably cheated.

Sometimes science or reasoning does not have the answer. I qualified in 1991 as a physical therapist, and within one year was working at the 1992 Barcelona Olympics with medal winners, without going through the standard apprenticeship of working my way up over a period of years. I just took it all in my stride.

Looking back now, I can see how I succeeded so quickly: I was more driven, more enthusiastic, more passionate and more talented as a physical therapist than I ever was as an athlete. It became my all-or-nothing, but with a difference. My previous all-or-nothing life was in the triathlon, yet that ended in one split second. When I lost that and found a career that I could excel in, I grabbed it with all my might, and worked harder and madder at it than anyone I knew. I understand why some people are sceptical about my success. For some people, especially fellow professionals who have earned their university degrees, their master's and PhD titles, and have theory-based education far more extensive than mine, it can be hard to fathom how an athlete can be one day competing on the international level and the next year be treating the best sporting flesh and bone in the world.

Life is full of little mysteries and that is what is so special about it. Everyone has been given talents and abilities. But each person has to tap into their own potential and exercise the choice to use them. As my good friend and esteemed Tyrone football manager Mickey Harte once stated: "The key to everything is to respect uniqueness. That is the thread that defines my teams, and maybe my entire outlook on life. To get the most from life and people, we must respect every individual for their talents and abilities. That is the baseline from which we can never go wrong."

When I was competing at international level in triathlon, people would often comment to me, "Ger, you're some man for punishment. I could never do it. All that training sounds too much like hard work." I would smile and reply, "I never see training as hard work. It's something I love doing." Every day I embraced the opportunity to push my body to new levels of performance.

People make similar comments to me about my career as a physical therapist: "Do you ever get tired? How do your hands keep going?

I could never do your job. It's too much like hard work." Again, I respond: "I love treating sportspeople and helping them to overcome their injuries and setbacks."

I prefer to see my role as a physical therapist as a calling, rather than work. My positive attitude towards what I do each day ensures I never get overtired or bored, or lose enthusiasm. I see many people who find their work tiring; they get burdened, bothered and physically and psychologically run down because their attitude towards what they do is that their job is "work", sometimes "hard work", and they find it stressful, instead of gaining some sense of fulfilment from it.

There are numerous scientific studies that support the claim that one's underlying attitude affects one's satisfaction and sense of fulfilment at work. Arguably the best research on attitude and general orientation towards work was a study conducted in 1997 by Dr Amy Wrzesniewski, an organisational psychologist and professor of business at New York University. She and her colleagues showed that workers are generally divided into three distinct categories:

- Group one view work as just a job. For them, the primary focus is on the financial rewards that the work brings. The nature of the work itself may hold little interest, pleasure or fulfilment for them.

- Group two view work as a career. Their primary focus is on advancement rather than financial motivation. These people are more motivated by prestige, social status, and the power that comes with titles and higher appointments at work. They may invest personally in the job, but as soon as the promotions stop they start to become dissatisfied. Their interest in the job can evaporate and they may seek new work to get back on the ladder towards reaching advancement.

- Group three are those who view their work as a calling. These individuals do the work for the sake of the work itself. They tend to love the work and, if they could afford to, they would continue doing the work even if they didn't get paid. They see their work as meaningful, having a higher purpose and making a contribution to society or to the world. Those that view the work as a calling tend to have significantly higher work satisfaction, as well as overall life satisfaction, than those who view work as a job or career.

Satisfaction with life and work is often more telling and important than income and occupational prestige. Some people spend years and years studying to train and qualify for a job or career that, after a couple of years, does not fulfil them. I studied Business Administration for four years to prepare to follow family tradition, yet after five years working in my family jewellery and optical business I became disillusioned with the work path I had chosen. It was not meaningful or purposeful, at least not for me, and I had the choice of sticking it out as a career that put food on the table and paid the bills, or to choose an alternative path that, to me, was more purposeful, meaningful and fulfilling. Change is never easy; some people stick to the mundane job and work because they lack the courage to change. It's easier to continue on the same path, becoming more dissatisfied, while using the crutch of excuses like "I hate my job but I have no other options" or "I'm too old now to change."

Almost every day of my life I meet people who are stuck in a rut, searching for options. I encourage people to follow their star and their instinct. Life is not a dress rehearsal. We pass through this world once and I encourage people to embrace the opportunity to do what they want to do with their life. I explain that I am an example of someone who did not find his calling the conventional way. I did not go through the standard four-year university education to become a standard physiotherapist. I found an alternative, and qualified as a sports physical therapist – proof, perhaps, that where there is a will there is a way.

22

Making the Transition from Sport to Life

Some people who are successful in sport can later be like a lost ship at sea when it comes to life. What made them succeed in sport somehow seems to elude them in the field they chose after sport. Most have not registered that the ingredients that made them successful in an individual or team sport can easily be transferred to make them equally successful in another endeavour.

If the drive, passion and the belief is transferred to their study, to their career and to their family life, they can make them equally successful. The individual sportsperson, whether it's the long-distance runner or the triathlete or the athlete involved in some other single-minded pursuit, has learned the ability to do it alone; those in team sports have learned that no one person makes a team but that teamwork is the secret.

This principle of transference from sport to life is one that I truly believe in. Many successful athletes go on to become successful in life after sport. They have understood the principle of transference. Others, without sport and competition, can lose their drive and their willpower and this is obvious when you meet them. Their vitality is gone, as if they have accepted that their youth and good days have passed them by. Some of them have bought into a life without excitement and limited opportunity. The challenge for someone like this, an athlete successful in their sport, is to make a list of the qualities that made them successful in the first place. Once the ingredients are identified, it then becomes a question of attitude. With a positive attitude, the successful ingredients can be transferred and used to bring joy, success and happiness into work and family life. The alternative is a wasted life, full of drudge, insecurity and failed opportunity.

My good friend Bobby Behan, from Killenard in Co. Laois, is an example of a man who had a successful career as head of Oakley Eyewear in Ireland. Yet he packed in his secure job, with company car, to pursue his dream of competing for Ireland in triathlon at the 2008 Beijing Olympic Games. He relocated to South Africa to avail of excellent coaching and facilities. He funded his mission with some personal savings and limited sponsorship. He is one of the most up-beat, positive and enthusiastic people I know. But he had difficulty with injuries, and these soon scuppered his plans. One day he flew home to meet me, to see if there was anything further we could do to address his injuries. We discussed the pros and cons of pushing on and chasing his dream, but also weighed up the consequence of perhaps lifelong injury. We drew a line in the sand. Bobby retired from triathlon one day and the following day put his name back in the hat, job hunting, but knowing he wanted to somehow stay involved in sport.

He soon landed a job with Specialized, the giant US bicycle manufacturer. He brought his passion, enthusiasm and positivity to his job. Within a couple of years, his ability to transfer those ingredients from sport to life was noticed by the top management in Specialized. He now heads Specialized global sports marketing for mountain bike and triathlon. He still rides the bike most days, and is very happy and content in his new skin.

I, too, have entered the fascinating world of developiong sport technology. Sometime during my early teenage years I developed a fascination for and natural inquisitiveness about running shoes and competition spikes, and later that developed into an interest in performance bicycles and equipment. Whenever travelling abroad, I always headed to the local sports and bike shops, and spent hours examining and comparing the latest products on the market. I never lost the fascination and, indeed, it has given me the opportunity to work with leaders in the industry.

In my earliest running years, I ran a lot on grass, barefoot, because my coach at the time PJ O'Sullivan explained to me that barefoot running strengthens the sinews around the ankles. Later, when treating Kelly Holmes and seeing how injury prone she was, I could tell that one of the causative factors was wearing spiked shoes on the synthetic track. With that in mind, I designed a racing flat that was moulded onto a spike plate, which gave her more support but retained the traction on the wet synthetic track that can become slippery in wet conditions. Likewise, I determined that Paula Radcliffe did not need all the cushioning of a modern-day running shoe, as she was a fore-foot striker. What she needed was a more rigid midsole; with the soft midsole she was dissipating shock, and losing force.

In the quest to explore my many ideas in terms of running footwear, I re-visited the concept of barefoot technology, and Nike, the giant US athletic footwear company, contracted me for six years to work with their research and design team in Beaverton, Oregon. My approach to a running shoe was "less is more", a shoe that is more minimalistic than a standard athletic shoe, designed to cushion and stabilise the foot. However, this was controversial as, for over twenty years, the athletic footwear companies promoted the big, thick-soled shoes on the basis that cushioning and shock absorption was everything. Yet kinematic studies showed that athletic shoes that packaged, cushioned and protected the foot in fact resulted in a greater incidence of injuries in athletes. In effect, the shoe made the human foot redundant, akin to the person who wears a collar around their neck. The collar holds up the neck and the underlying neck muscles weaken as a result, similar to when a person breaks a leg and it is put into a plaster cast. Six weeks later, the cast is taken off, and the atrophy of the leg is sizeable.

Along with Nike, I developed the Nike Free shoe in 2004, which gained wide attention – and suddenly barefoot running and minimalistic shoes became very popular. These days I am aligned with the German footwear and sportswear giant Adidas. Never being far away from the latest research and technology, always being alert to the trends ahead, helps to keep my brain active.

In my triathlon days I was the first person in Europe to experiment with the time trial handlebars, while these days the so-called aero bar is now a necessity in time trials, triathlon and Ironman events. I also experimented with the five-spoke composite front wheel. While this made sense from an aerodynamic perspective, the wheel was too heavy and never made an impact. Some things work, other things fail, but it's always important to push the barriers in terms of technology.

Even though my competitive days are behind me, I remain every bit as excited by technology and equipment. Specialized supply me with their inventions to receive my feedback, and their latest time trial bike – the Specialized Shiv – is the fastest and most technologically aerodynamic bike ever designed. I ride it to give informed feedback, and to keep abreast of the latest developments in the pursuit of legal higher, faster and stronger athletic performance.

When Paul Kimmage was competing in the 1989 Tour de France, extracting every ounce of energy out of his body and digging deep into his willpower to survive the tough days in the French Pyrenees and Alps, he was already using the ingredients that made him an Irish road race champion and Olympic cyclist. After each stage, he would sit down and pen the day's activity, recounting the drama, the excitement and the pain – and created a unique insight into the peloton. These were his honest and true feelings, as experienced by himself, a mere *domestique* – or team journeyman – trying to eke a living out of cycling and to survive in the toughest three-week grand tour of them all.

These daily accounts from the Tour de France were first published in the late and lamented *Sunday Tribune* newspaper. They were carried across a full two-page spread and made for gripping reading. The professional cyclist turning the pedals in the Tour de France was unaware that his account was top-class material. After the Tour, he was offered a full-time job as a feature writer for the *Sunday Tribune*. He made the transfer from professional athlete to professional writer almost automatically. As it happened, he was a born writer, the best sports feature writer that I have read. He is now the chief sports writer for the *Sunday Times* and has won numerous Writer of the Year awards for his work. I purchase the *Sunday Times* each week just to read his features.

It is amazing how one life ends and another life starts. I now respect why Paul Kimmage asked me in 1991 if I took performance-enhancing drugs to fuel my triathlon performances: he was the ultimate professional, doing his job to the best of his ability and ensuring he had looked under every stone.

Four years later, in 1995, Paul Kimmage contacted me again. This time he came to visit me. He travelled to Teddington, London, where I was based for the summer months as a physical therapist. We did not mention my previous triathlon life or his cycling exploits. He sat in a small room for hours, just observing me applying my trade. He was a fly on the wall, watching me treating many of the great Kenyan athletes of the time. At 7.00 p.m. we mounted two old bicycles and tried to follow a group of gazelle-like Kenyan athletes as they ran the seven-mile lap of Bushy Park. The gazelles were too fleet of foot. We soon got bogged down in the rough grass, and stopped and laughed in awe as the Kenyan athletes legged it off into the distance. Here we were, two former athletes that once competed at the highest level in our respective sports, and we were not able to keep up.

Paul Kimmage penned the following feature article, which appeared in the *Sunday Independent* on August 13, 1995:

THE MAN THEY CALL DAKTARI

"Agghhhhhh."

We join them in a small room of 59 Park Road, Teddington, London. William Sigei, the fastest 10,000 metres runner in the world, is in pain. A lot of pain. He felt the twinge in his hamstring during training and went to see "Daktari" straight away. Why? Because that's what you do when you've got an injury.

You go to his room and knock on the door. He runs his palms over the damage, takes out his pot of Tiger Balm and..."agggghhhhh"...goes to work straight away.

This is how it looks to the fly on the wall. The black man with the sore leg is lying on the treatment couch. The white man standing over him appears to be giving a massage, but William is not enjoying it.

Daktari's great white thumbs are pressing too forcefully into the area giving him pain and it's hurting. It is hurting bad. He turns and grabs Daktari's arm and pleads for leniency: "Aghhh, very pain, very pain." But, Daktari is having none of it.

"Tough, my friend, isn't it? But just let me stay on it for a little bit longer."

Gerard Hartmann from Limerick remembers a time when he used to rise at 5.00 a.m. Triathlon was his drug and, in order to be competitive, he had to squeeze his daily training around his 9.00 a.m. to 5.00 p.m. job. He would get out of bed and pull on his togs. Then pull off his togs and put on his suit. Then pull off his suit and pull on his runners. Then pull off his runners and go to bed. A monastic lifestyle? No, he never looked at it like that. Seven times the National Champion, 14th in the

World Championships; no sacrifice was too great when the target was the summit. He never reached it...but believes he just might now.

Gerard Hartmann remembers the day when his life changed. It was 1987 and, crossing a railway line on his bike, he came down and hit the ground hard. He woke the following morning with a searing pain in his back and hip. The swimming was put on "hold", and the running and the bike.

For the next fourteen months he limped up and down the country in search of a medicinal cure. Fourteen months of specialists taught a man a lot about his oil and nuts and bolts. The more he found out, the more he wanted to know. He was neck high in theory books and manuals and it still wasn't enough. He wanted to wield a "spanner". He wanted to be a "mechanic".

Abandoning his post at the head of a family jewellery business that had spanned four generations (he is an only son), he travelled to Gainesville, Florida in 1989 and took a degree in physical therapy. Once qualified, he set himself up in a clinic in Gainesville – Florida Sports Medicine and Orthopaedic Centre. Today, he is rated among the best and "guru" to the rich and famous.

We join him in a small room at 59 Park Road. He has come to London and the quaint suburb of Teddington, at the invitation of the world famous agent Kim McDonald, who has hired him on a twelve-week contract to look after his stable of runners.

Moses Kiptanui, the world record holder in the steeplechase and 5,000m, has just slipped through his fingers. William Sigei is on the table as we speak. Eighty per cent of McDonald's athletes are Kenyan. They have a name for the Irish "musungo" (white man). He is the man they call Daktari.

"Aghhhhhhhhhhhhhh." "Most physiotherapists," explains Hartmann, digging his thumbs deep into Sigei, "use a more passive style – gentle with the hands on, ultrasound, laser and electro-stimulation machines, hydrotherapy, ice and heat. I tend to be aggressive with my hands and do a lot of manipulative work. William, for example, has a hamstring strain. In two weeks he hopes to break the world record, so, I have got to get him right and on time. What I am trying to do is increase the pliability of the tissue using manual therapy. It sounds contradictory, but I am going in very deep on tissue that is already tender to...."

His explanation is interrupted by a knock on the door. Another Kenyan with an injury sticks his head through the gap and requests treatment. "Wait downstairs. I'll be looking at you soon," he is told. (Although Daktari has some words of Swahili he prefers to speak to his Kenyan patients in Johnny Weissmuller – "Me Tarzan" – English.) "Now where were we?" he asks. "Surely by going in deeply you are only making his hamstring more sore?" He shakes his head. "Think of it like this. Anytime there is a trauma of the tissue, the body tries to heal it with scar tissue (a substance known as collagen). Now scar tissue I would liken to a blob of chewing gum that has been walked into the carpet – we need to get it out to make the carpet clean again. But how do we do it? Do we take the quickest way and use a hammer and chisel? Or, do we use hot water and try to melt it away? Well effectively, I suppose, I am going about it with a hammer and chisel, but in a very specific scientific meticulous way." "Aghhhhhhhhh."

We leave them in a small room at 59 Park Road. The Blackman. The Whiteman. The chewing gum. The carpet. Next time you get injured, Gerard Hartmann knows a way.

23

Positivity and Drive in the Face of Adversity

Noel Carroll rang me out of the blue one morning, like he so often did, only this time it was a phone call I will never forget. It was a Friday, October 23, 1998, and he was looking for some advice to pass on to his daughter Nicola. She was living in Barcelona at the time and had sustained a minor knee injury while in training to run a local 10 kilometre road race. I told him to make sure she took it easy, to ice it regularly and not to run through any serious pain.

Noel thanked me, and finished the conversation by saying he was about to leave his office in Dublin, where he worked as CEO of the Dublin Chamber of Commerce, and drive the short distance to the UCD campus at Belfield, where he acted as coach to the university athletics team.

There, he joined a young scholarship athlete named Andrew Walker, and together they would share the four-mile lunchtime run around the sports fields and wooded paths of Belfield.

Noel wasn't just a great coach; he was also a wonderful philosopher, and always worked on developing the mind of his athletes as well as their physical fitness. This leisurely run was to be the start of a promising weekend: that evening he was set to drive his wife Deirdre O'Callaghan, the renowned Irish harpist, to the Wexford Opera Festival.

At the start of the run, Noel told the young Andrew Walker that he should go into Eason's in Dublin and purchase a book named *Jonathan Livingston Seagull* by Richard Bach. The popular small book, a mere 87 pages in length, is one of the most celebrated inspirational fables of our time, and as relevant today as it's ever been.

The run continued, and the chat, as always, had Noel acting as coach and mentor, guiding his small athletic flock. Once finished and standing next to Noel's Rover car, parked at the UCD sports centre, Andrew asked, "Noel, what is the name of that book again?"

Noel looked at him and replied, "*Jonathan Living...*" and before he had the full name spoken he suddenly dropped to the ground.

Noel Carroll, husband, father, champion runner and Olympian, coach, author, and one of the driving forces behind the starting of the Dublin City Marathon – and above all a truly special man – had dropped dead on the spot. He was a fit, superbly athletic 57-year old. He had taught so much to so many people, and he was a true role model.

Noel Carroll's sudden death sent shockwaves through the athletic community. It was greeted with disbelief mainly, but also great sadness. Some said it was Jim Fixx all over again – the American runner and author who also died suddenly at the height of the running boom in the 1980s. The small minority of people who doubt the benefits of running could say, "That running business will kill you." Who knows? But if Jim Fixx and Noel Carroll, and my friend Kim McDonald who also died of a sudden heart attack at 45 years of age, had not exercised, maybe they would have died years younger.

All I know is that, from almost 40 years of swimming, running, cycling and all-round exercising, I personally feel good and function well when I keep fit. On some occasions, when I have been sidelined through injury or illness or have been too busy with work commitments, my zest drops and I start to chug. There is absolutely no doubt in my mind that regular exercise has positive benefits that far outweigh the risks involved.

Within days of Noel's death, and still dazed by his sudden passing, I pledged my support to the young Andrew Walker, taking him under my wing and offering to help him with his athletics and career in whatever way I could.

A couple of weeks after Noel's death, when Andrew was visiting me in Limerick and recalling the last moments he had with his coach, he explained about the book *Jonathan Livingston Seagull*. There and then, we walked together up to Eason's in Limerick and purchased two copies. That evening I read it from cover to cover, in one sitting, and realised how the story and message were indeed so simple. I saw how I shared many of the traits of Jonathan Livingston Seagull. In some ways we were brothers in the flight in pursuit of excellence. Here is a synopsis of the book:

For the flocks and flocks of seagulls that you see by the shore, life consists of the mundane routine of eating and surviving. Flying is just the means of finding food. Jonathan Livingston Seagull is different. He is no ordinary seagull. For him flying is the most important thing in life, and perfecting it like no other gull has ever done. Against the conventions of his flock and the greater seagull society, he seeks to find a higher purpose and his mantra is to become the best at what he loves. Jonathan has no fear of learning. To reach excellence he will make mistakes along the way but he sees no limits and he learns at a tremendous rate.

Jonathan chooses to be a one-in-a-million bird. The most important thing for him is living to reach out and touch perfection in doing what he loves to do, and that is to fly. He spends hour after hour every day practising flight, testing advanced aeronautics. Jonathan can see that other seagulls' lives consist of boredom and fear and anger. That is the reason they are unfulfilled and their lives are so short.

Jonathan perfects flight and sets a world speed record for seagulls. But it is at a price. He knows that "The gull sees farthest who flies highest." The flock on the ground stand squawking and fighting among themselves, wasting unnecessary time and energy.

Jonathan's pursuit of excellence does not make him popular with other birds. He is reprimanded for his pursuit of excellence. He is called into a Council Gathering by the elder seagulls and is brought to "stand to centre" for shame. He is told he violated "the dignity and tradition of the Gull Family". He is cast out by his own gull society, banished to a solitary life on the Far Cliffs.

Jonathan pleads to the Council flock: "Give me one chance, let me show you what I've found…Who is more responsible than a gull who finds and follows a meaning, a higher purpose for life. For thousands of years we have squabbled after fish heads, but now we have a reason to live – to learn, to discover to be free."[5] It falls on deaf ears. The gulls

---

[5] Richard Bach, *Jonathan Livingston Seagull: A Story*, London: HarperElement, 2003, p. 25.

intone together, and with one accord solemnly close their ears and turn their backs on Jonathan.

Jonathan spends the rest of his days chasing excellence. His one sorrow is not solitude, it is that other gulls refuse to believe the glory of flight that awaits them, that they refuse to open their eyes and see.

When I was a student at the Salesian College in Pallaskenry, Co. Limerick, showing enthusiasm and potential as a young runner, I was fortunate that I had a Sports master, Fr Martin Loftus, who gave me the freedom to expand my wings to fly. As a special concession, he allowed me to get up early and run before breakfast. Fr Loftus looked out for his flock of sportsmen in true Salesian Christian fashion. St John Bosco, founder of the Salesian Order, had stated: "The teacher who is seen in the classroom and nowhere else is a teacher and nothing more; but let him go with his boys to recreation and sport and he becomes a brother."

To me, this freedom of running was like a powerful light that I could switch on during the dark winter mornings and evenings. It was a floodlight that lit up the field that I shared with sheep. I sometimes ran barefoot on the field at night, like Jonathan training and perfecting what I loved, spurred on by the bright glow of passion for running.

I was also fortunate that I had parents who encouraged me to chase my dreams. In 1978, at sixteen years of age, months after I ran a marathon fundraising for Trocáire, I won the All-Ireland 2,000-metre Steeplechase Under-17 title; the following day I finished second in the 800-metre event. That Sunday evening, I set off on a ferry from Rosslare to Cherbourg in France with my friend Derek Wallace, who had finished second to me in the steeplechase.

I had planned to cycle almost 3,000 miles around Europe. Derek bailed out after one week and got a train back to Cherbourg and the ferry home.

I continued on my merry way, covering 2,700 miles in 6 weeks, cycling the length of France and through northern Italy, Switzerland and Germany. Doing such extreme things at a young age set me apart and gave me the confidence and independence that would serve me well throughout life.

When I arrived back in Limerick after my cycling tour, my dad greeted me with great relief. When I had not been in contact for over three weeks, my mother feared the worst and had travelled to Lourdes to pray for my safe return.

It can't have been easy for my parents to see their only son go to the US at 17 years of age to pursue excellence in running, instead of continuing a long tradition and working in the family business; head off a second time to pursue excellence in triathlon; and, at 29 years of age, change tack again and return to college in the US for further study.

I was fortunate, too, to have stumbled across the emerging sport of triathlon, all of 30 years ago, in 1981. Triathlon and Ironman gave me more than I could ever have imagined: it gave me freedom and identity, and it allowed me to taste sporting success. It also taught me discipline and how to endure the pain and suffering necessary to reach the top. It gave me plenty of highs and, indeed, lows, introduced me to so many people, and helped me make some great friends. It allowed me the opportunity to chase excellence. Nobody ever wins the race of excellence: it is an ongoing process, a race that never stops. In many ways, excellence is perseverance in disguise. Most important of all, sport and triathlon gave me the confidence to believe in myself. Sport builds and tests character like nothing else I know.

Like Jonathan Livingston Seagull, I, too, have come across my detractors. In the early years doing triathlon, some people tried to tell me it was only a "fad" or a "craze", a sport that would not last. Some actually scorned it, stating that it was only a sport for failed athletes who could not succeed in an individual sport: "You could not make it in athletics, so you are trying to make a go of this crazy sport" – well, I heard that a few times. Yet, to a certain degree, that comment is correct: many of the top triathlon stars have been good in a single discipline, either swimming, cycling or running, but not quite top class.

It can be true that a combination of adequate talents can lead to excellence. It was Larry Mullen Jnr, the drummer with the band U2, who explained to me that as a drummer he is very good, but there are other drummers in the world just as good, if not better. And the same with the Edge, the guitarist, and Adam Clayton, the bass guitar player – there are probably other guitarists in the world just as good as them too. But, together with Bono, if you put these four band members together, as Larry admitted, "Something very, very special happens." Magic – in other words. Together, as a group, they light up and rock the world, and they have done so for over 30 years now. To this day, they are reaching higher, searching for more.

Colin Jackson, the British former sprint and hurdling athlete, once commented to me that in a flat-out 100-metre sprint there are at least 40 athletes in the world who could beat him. But he perfected clearing 10 hurdles in the 110 metres hurdle event to become a world record holder and two-time world champion. To his natural speed he added great hurdling skill and technique to become a world beater.

There will always be the doubters, either negative people or those with big chips on their shoulders. There is no good whatsoever in negativity. It is a soul destroyer, drains people of their vitality and robs them of their potential in life.

Jack O'Connor, the successful manager of the Kerry football team, once told me what he thought of negativity. "I don't do negativity," he said. "There are two types of people in this world: those who fill your bucket and those who drain your bucket. Some people who drain your bucket like to turn it upside down to make sure it's completely empty. They are to be avoided. But the worst of all are those that drain your bucket drip by bloody drip. They're the worst type of all because they suck you dry, unknown to yourself."

Of course, there are people who suck themselves dry too, by wallowing in their own misery. One individual, a physiotherapist, who must have a particularly large chip on his shoulder, appears to be consumed with anger and jealousy at the success I have had in my profession. In fact, he has disparaged me enough times to keep a solicitor busy for weeks. With every chance, he tells people that I am not adequately qualified. He has written to heads of university departments, and often, having read an article in which I am featured, he immediately complains to the person who wrote it. To me, he is either wasting his energy on a nonsensical battle that can never be won or else he is tormented by his own shortcomings. One should never let what they cannot do or affect get in the way of what they can do. The higher one flies the more one can see, and the more jealous people get and want to see them fail.

I don't waste energy on these negative impositions. Instead, I set my stall out to reach new heights, to excel and to continue chasing excellence. I let my work and performance speak for itself. My client base tells me all I need to know about what success really is. I focus on them, not on the competition.

In life, there is endless potential. I didn't come into this world to be a magpie sitting on the fence or, worse still, a bickering seagull. I came to participate, not to be a spectator.

To reach the top, not just in sport but in business or in life, you have to think outside the box and take risks. You have to believe in yourself through thick and thin. Anything worthwhile in life is gained through hard work and sacrifice.

The goal should be to reach beyond yourself, to aspire to go where no one else has ventured, and the end result will, more often than not, be success and happiness. Extend yourself to sharing with others, reach out to the greater cause and join the brotherhood of mankind – those who lead the flock in the right direction.

When Jonathan Livingston Seagull attempts to come back to the flock, there is a great clamour of squawks and screeches from the thousands of seagulls: "He is a devil! DEVIL! Come to break the Flock!"

> "Why is it," Jonathan puzzled, "that the hardest thing in the world is to convince a bird that he is free, and that he can prove it for himself if he'd just spend a little time practicing? Why should that be so hard?"

The following morning the flock has forgotten its insanity and Jonathan's seagull friend Seagull Fletcher enquires: "Jonathan, remember what you said a long time ago about loving the Flock enough to return to it and help it to learn?...I don't understand how you manage to love a mob of birds that has tried to kill you."

Jonathan replies, "...You don't love hatred and evil...You have to practice and see the real gull, the good in every one of them, and to help them see it in themselves. That's what I mean by love. It's fun, when you get the knack of it."[6]

Mastering something that you are passionate about – now, that is a worthwhile pursuit! No matter what it is that interests you, follow your star and your star only. Believe in yourself, have fun with it and look out on your travels for the Jonathan Livingston Seagulls of this world.

---

[6] Bach, *Jonathan Livingston Seagull*, pp. 84–85.

Paula Radcliffe is one of those special people. A few years ago, Keith Wood and his wife Nicola invited Paula and me to their home in Killaloe for dinner. Nicola joked that her claim to fame was leading against Paula in an under-11 race – for the first 200 yards at least! Amid the fun and banter, Keith silenced up for a few moments, leaving us in suspense. Then he quietly said, "Paula, I never thought you'd make it. You were always just losing out. How did you go from being second best to becoming a winner?"

A little gobsmacked by the candid appraisal from this giant of world rugby, Paula reddened, paused to compose herself, and, eyes beaming, said: "Keith, coming from this small village of Killaloe, how did you make it?"

Paula Radcliffe has won World Championship titles at cross country and in the marathon. She has a world marathon record of 2 hours, 15 minutes and 25 seconds, which is arguably the best and the cleanest world record in women's athletics. Paula knows that the gull that flies highest sees farthest.

On the treatment table of my practice, I work on every sinew of muscle. I also align Paula's back and her neck, mobilise her ankle joints and, most of all, I treat her mind. An elite, highly tuned athlete like Paula Radcliffe knows who trusts her and who believes in her ability. Any weakness in my armour, any lack of confidence and belief in her on my part, she can sense. Of course, small doubts always creep in. Most of these doubts are insecurities, sometimes to do with myself and not in the athlete. Will I serve her well? Have I enough tools in my box to ensure she goes to the starting line healthy in mind, body and spirit?

Paula and I share one thing in common: we are both ultimate perfectionists. We need to tick off the boxes, to ensure that no stone is left unturned in our quest for success. The athlete and physical therapist can sometimes become an amalgam in the quest for perfection, in the pursuit of winning. The pessimists will always fight and argue among themselves, already ringing the doom bell of failure: "No way, no way can Radcliffe win an Olympic medal in 2012 at almost 39 years of age, in her fifth Olympics. She was like a gull with a broken flapping wing in Beijing, running on one leg, and in Athens she broke down at

23 miles with the stadium within sight and a medal within grasp. No way, no way..."

It's not our place to judge and to doubt others. Kelly Holmes was cast aside as finished and costing the British Athletic Association too much money, with no return for their investment. Yet she delivered a bronze medal in the 800 metres at the Sydney Olympics at 30 years of age. She also knew that, given a healthy chance, she could deliver even more. At 34 years of age, winning the 800 metres and 1,500 metres at the Athens Olympics was not only evidence of the power of her self-belief, but was also a slap in the face to those who had doubted her.

Sometimes the pursuit of excellence does not make you popular with others. But if more people believed in the glory that awaits them, if they opened their eyes to see the potential and talents in themselves and to put them to use for self and a greater cause, then the world as a whole could only be a better place. As the physically weak man can make himself strong by careful and patient training, so, too, the man of weak mind can make it strong by exercising the right way of thinking, and practising the art of believing in the self and understanding that anything is possible.

People who take their life and talents for granted underachieve. I need no other stimulus to value every day, to respect my life and my health, than when I think of my nine friends who took their own lives. Nine suicides: nine lost lives. I remember, also, my friends and comrades who tragically lost their lives off their road bikes, out doing what they enjoyed best: Tadg Howell, Cork; Joseph Kelly, Carrick-on-Suir, Co. Tipperary; Joey Hannan, Croom, Co. Limerick; Davy McCaul, Belfast; Tony O'Regan, Limerick; Caroline Kearney, Dublin.

Every single moment of every day is valued more and more when I cannot pick up the phone and speak to the following friends who impacted my life. Their lives were snatched away through illness or sudden death: Fanahan McSweeney, Cork; Ann Kearney, Noel Carroll and Brendan O'Reilly, Dublin; Pat Curley and Tom Staunton, Sligo; Kim McDonald, Teddington, London; Laurent Fignon, Paris; Solomon Ori-Orison, Galway; Christy O'Brien, Tony Purtill, Fr Frank Madden, John O'Donnell, Gerry Ryan and Tim O'Brien, Limerick; Grete Waitz, Oslo, Norway; and Keith Iovine, New Orleans, US.

Of the over 300 Kenyan athletes I have known, the following also died way too young: Richard Chelimo, Luka Kipkoech, Lucas Sang, David Lelei, Sammy Lagat and Paul Kipkoech.

All of these people are with me in my life's work, in my travels and in my prayers, and serve as a reminder that we all come into this world as participators, not spectators.

Tomorrow will bring its own challenges and opportunities. The only way I know is to chase excellence and fly higher to see and achieve more. Every day alive is God's gift. Take it from me – life is precious. Today, everyday, embrace it.

EPILOGUE

The pursuit of excellence never ends. To reach the top in any endeavour, in sport, in business or in life in general, one must always be willing to learn. Lifelong learning and lifelong striving to do things the best you possibly can ensures that you avoid stagnation, and stay competitive and fresh.

It was Friday, June 18, 2009. I left Limerick at 6.00 a.m. and drove the two hours to Ireland's longest beach at Inch Strand on the Dingle Peninsula. The beach was completely empty – there wasn't a soul in sight except for me and my footprints on the sand. I walked in a pensive mood for almost an hour, readying myself for the task ahead. I was getting my mind focused and into the zone for a challenge of a crazy sort, all on my own. Once again, I was exploring my own physical, mental and suffering capabilities towards the reward of conquering and achieving what I mapped out to do in a far tougher challenge two weeks later.

I geared up and rolled out of sleepy Inch a little after 9.00 a.m., cycling five miles back towards Castlemaine before turning onto a narrow road barely the width of a van. Facing me was a near vertical two-mile climb, which dropped down into the village of Camp and on to Stradbally. After that, the route led to the base of Ireland's highest pass, the Conor Pass, some one hour and twenty minutes into the cycle. I mentally prepared myself for the penance ahead. From the Stradbally side to the top of the Conor Pass is three miles of climbing, a climb that puts most car engines into overheat. From Dingle back up to the top it is four steep miles, and on wet, misty days you cycle in the surreal mist, high up above civilisation.

On this day, I cycled the Conor Pass three times from each side, a total of 21 miles of gut-wrenching and muscle-aching pedalling, and without ever dismounting the bike. I arrived back at a busy Inch beach after cycling for six hours and twenty minutes, packed the bike into my car and drove home. When I came in the door, my wife Diane said, "How was your day?" "Good," I said. "I had a nice cycle and I'm ready for the Marmotte."

Always trying to soar high to see farthest, I was going outside my own day-to-day comfortable routine of standing at a physio table, treating flesh and bone. I was going out into the unknown, taking a push bike up into the highest mountains, to try to understand a little more about life and about myself. This is something I can never do when smothered with the hustle and bustle of business, clinic life and taking care of other people's problems and needs. We all need freedom to find our true self.

The Marmotte – or Marmotte L'Équipe Du Grand Trophee Randonneur, to give it its full title – is a beast of an event. It is one of the toughest one-day cycling events on the globe. Some 9,000 cyclists from all over the world take part, real cycling purists – and you need to be as it's a 174-kilometre hell of an event that makes even cycling the Conor Pass six times in one go seem insignificant. Preparation, preparation, preparation has always been my mantra, and the cornerstone of my success in everything I do. The Conor Pass served a purpose. I cycled the Marmotte in the spirit of the Jonathan Livingston Seagulls of this world, pushing my boundaries and enjoying the day's experience into the bargain.

The Marmotte presents the most famous of famous Alpine climbs, used over the years in the Tour de France, which open the chest and make the lungs gasp for oxygen. The first climb of the day, the Col du Glandon, is nine miles of climbing, the second, the Col du Télégraphe is eleven miles, and the third, the famous Col du Galibier, is fourteen miles of climbing; together they make up eight hours of cycling. Then you face one of the most infamous climbs in cycling history – the Alpe d'Huez, a nine-mile climb up 21 hairpin bends to the summit and the finish line of the Marmotte. Awaiting me at the top was a gold medal that I won for the 45–50-year-old category.

To win something is always nice, but the victory I chase at this stage of life is the uniqueness of being healthy and totally alive and appreciating that every day is a gift. I still want to participate in this life and give my best in the pursuit of excellence. In that regard, perhaps I was born to perform, but sport remains my lifelong friend. Sport can save; sport can heal – and that's the lesson for us all. Let sport shape your life.

Triathlon – From Sporting Craze to Ireland's Fastest Growing Sport

By Ian O'Riordan

People who take part in triathlons will tell you they are primarily motivated by health and fitness. But that simply isn't true. For all the cheap thrills at our fingertips these days, most of us lead pretty dull lives, and, bored with our daily routines, set out to find something a little less ordinary.

The golf course might be alright for some, and good luck to them; for others, motivated by fearlessness and a little craziness, it is swimming, cycling and running – and preferably in quick succession. This is what gets the adrenaline pumping for the proper life junkie, and if it helps keep the arteries free of cholesterol then that's a mere side-effect.

When Gerard Hartmann unwittingly and utterly naively walked into this strange and unusual pursuit, in Lake Charles, Louisiana, sometime in the spring of 1981, there was no way he could possibly have imagined it would someday become one of the headline events at the Olympic Games – and a mass participation event, on a massive scale. But then, who could have imagined this?

The truth is, some people still can't make sense of the triathlon: the zipping and stripping of wetsuits – Orca, 2XU, Zoot; the clipping into and dismounting of bicycles – Cervelo, Pinarello, Cannondale; the lightweight flats and half-naked running... No wonder Nike keep coming up with such catchy slogans.

Perhaps the triathlon will only ever make sense to those who have tried it. What is certain is that the triathlon is among the fastest growing sports in the free world, and Ireland is no exception. Gerard Hartmann took his experience from Lake Charles that day and forged not just a new life, but a new lifestyle – and if Ireland now boasts several world-class triathlons, from Kilkee to Tri-Athy to Tri-Athlone, every single one of them owes a little nod to the original of the species, and Hartmann is unquestionably among them.

Ever since making its Olympic debut in Sydney in 2000, triathlon has continued to grow at all levels – from the very elite right on down to the amateur. The Olympic distance – a 1.5-kilometre swim, 40-kilometre cycle and 10-kilometre run – has also become the standard, although for most aspiring triathletes there is the standard sprint distance: a .75-kilometre swim, 20-kilometre cycle and 5-kilometre run.

At the elite end, Ireland is now, in the sporting parlance, punching above its weight. In Beijing in 2008, Emma Davis became Ireland's first Olympic representative, and both Gavin Noble, from Enniskillen, and Aileen Morrison, from Derry, are well within the world ranking range to compete in London in 2012. Morrison came late into the sport, having started out as a swimmer, yet, like many triathletes, soon found herself thoroughly addicted.

There were 140 triathlons on the Irish calendar in 2011, and Triathlon Ireland now boasts over 5,500 members and active clubs in every county. Recently it secured its first major sponsorship with a three-year deal with Vodafone. It's estimated that over 16,000 people of all ages, gender and ability participated in a triathlon in 2011. The large growth in female participants, with a 60:40 male-to-female ratio, is perhaps one further reason why all the government health warnings have finally convinced us that, instead of taking up one sport, we should take up three at a time.

Come June 2012, the top 55 ranked international triathletes, men and women, will be nominated for the London Olympics, based on their 14 best results over the previous 2-year period. Ireland's Aileen Morrison and Gavin Noble are poised to make their Olympic debuts.

For more information and all Irish club listings see: www. triathlonireland.com.